QUESTIONS & ANSWERS:
ADMINISTRATIVE LAW

QUESTIONS & ANSWERS: ADMINISTRATIVE LAW

Multiple Choice and Short-Answer Questions and Answers

Second Edition

RUSSELL L. WEAVER
Professor of Law & Distinguished University Scholar
University of Louisville
Louis D. Brandeis School of Law

KAREN A. JORDAN
Professor of Law
University of Louisville
Louis D. Brandeis School of Law

ISBN: 978–1–4224–7710–6

NOTE TO USERS

To ensure that you are using the latest materials available in this area, please be sure to periodically check the LexisNexis Law School web site for downloadable updates and supplements at www.lexisnexis.com/lawschool.

Editorial Offices
121 Chanlon Rd., New Providence, NJ 07974 (908) 464-6800
201 Mission St., San Francisco, CA 94105-1831 (415) 908-3200
www.lexisnexis.com

MATTHEW◆BENDER

DEDICATION

To Ben and Kate with Love, RLW

ABOUT THE AUTHORS

Russell L. Weaver is Professor of Law and Distinguished University Scholar at the University of Louisville, Louis D. Brandeis School of Law. During his twenty-three years at the University of Louisville, he has visited at a number of U.S. law schools, having been invited to hold the Judge Spurgenon Bell Distinguished Professorship at the South Texas College of Law, and the Herbert Herff Chair of Excellence at the University of Memphis, Cecil C. Humphreys School of Law. In addition, he regularly visits at a number of foreign schools including the University of Montpellier, Faculty of Law, Montpellier, France, and the Johannes Guttenburg University, Faculty of Law, Mainz, Germany. He has also visited at law schools in England, Canada, Japan and Australia.

Professor Weaver has taught administrative law for more than twenty years. In addition, he has authored or co-authored scores of books and articles, including one of the leading administrative law casebooks, W. Funk, S. Shapiro & R. Weaver, *Administrative Procedure & Practice* (West, 2d ed., 2001). He has written numerous administrative law articles and is the organizer of the Administrative Law Discussion Forum.

Karen A. Jordan is a Professor of Law at the Brandeis School of Law at the University of Louisville. Professor Jordan teaches primarily in the areas of civil procedure, evidence, and administrative law. Her scholarly endeavors focus predominantly on regulatory law and policy issues, especially as they relate to the allocation of power between the federal and state systems. Professor Jordan's articles have appeared in leading journals, and have been cited in federal and state judicial opinions and course textbooks.

Professor Jordan has developed her administrative law expertise primarily in the health law arena. In the past, Professor Jordan has been a speaker at national conferences sponsored by the American Society of Law, Medicine and Ethics and the Association of American Law Schools; and has contributed to forums such as West Legal News and the employee benefits section of the Association of American Law Schools. More recently, she has focused on issues relating to judicial deference to agency actions and agency preemption.

PREFACE

Administrative Law covers issues relating to the authority and functioning of administrative agencies. What procedures must agencies follow? What rights must they accord to those affected by its action? Administrative Law also addresses issues relating to the relationship between courts and administrative agencies, and judicial review of agency action.

The purpose of this book is to test your understanding of administrative law and procedure, and to assist you in preparing for an administrative law exam. This book is not intended to provide a comprehensive explanation of administrative law concepts but as a supplement to class materials.

This book examines the major administrative law topics and concludes with a comprehensive Practice Final Exam. It includes an introduction to the study of administrative law and the Administrative Procedure Act, as well as such topics as rulemaking procedures, adjudication procedures and due process, retroactivity, non-legislative rules, reviewability, agency structure, inspections, reports, subpoenas, the Freedom of Information Act, and Attorneys Fees.

As you utilize these Questions, remember that there may not be a single correct answer, but there might be a "best answer." In other words, you might be asked to make informed judgments based on your knowledge of administrative law and your wisdom.

Professor Russell L. Weaver
Professor Karen A. Jordan
Louisville, Kentucky
May, 2010

TABLE OF CONTENTS

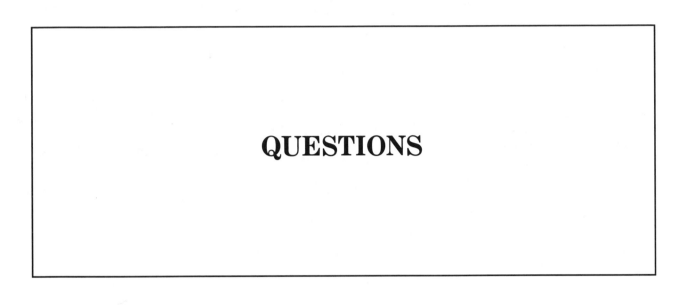

QUESTIONS

The Administrative Procedure Act is hereafter referred to as the "APA."

1.1. Regarding the history of administrative law, which of the following is an accurate statement?

    (A) The administrative state did not exist before President Roosevelt's New Deal legislative agenda of the 1930s.

    (B) The APA was enacted as part of the New Deal agenda, to help facilitate the rise of the administrative state.

    (C) During the New Deal era, judicial review of agency action eroded and the APA was enacted in response to concerns about increasing unfairness in the administrative process.

    (D) The New Deal led to a significant decrease in the number and power of administrative agencies and the APA was enacted to empower administrative agencies.

1.2. Identify and describe the types of agency proceedings expressly recognized by the APA.

The Northern Spotted Owl has been listed as a threatened species under the Endangered Species Act (ESA). The Bureau of Land Management (BLM) wishes to make timber sales on certain land within its jurisdiction, but has determined that logging would jeopardize the owl. The ESA prohibits federal agencies from taking any action that would jeopardize a listed species unless they obtain an exemption from the Endangered Species Committee (ESC). The ESC is comprised of six members who are heads of various interested agencies (Department of the Interior, Department of Agriculture, the Army, the Council on Economic Advisors, the EPA, and the National Oceanic and Atmospheric Administration), and one person appointed by the President to represent the affected State. An exemption may be granted only if the ESC determines that several statutory requirements are satisfied. BLM has petitioned for an exemption.

ANSWER:

1.3. In determining whether to grant the exemption, must the ESC follow procedures in the APA?

    (A) The ESC need not follow the APA because the ESC is not an agency.

(B) The ESC need not follow the APA because the proceeding involves matter relating to public property.

(C) The ESC need not follow the APA because the determination represents a general statement of policy.

(D) The ESC must follow the APA.

1.4. Assume that the ESC determines that the statutory requirements are not satisfied and thus that BLM is not entitled to an exemption. Regarding that determination, which of the following is a correct statement?

(A) The determination is a "rule" because the determination has only a future effect.

(B) The determination is an "order" because the determination is a type of licensing.

(C) The determination is not an "agency action" because it is neither a "final rule" nor a "final order."

(D) The determination is "relief" because it is neither a "final rule" nor a "final order."

1.5. Regarding economic justification for administrative regulation, which of the following is NOT an accurate statement?

(A) Administrative agencies generally should address problems associated with natural monopolists through price and profit regulation.

(B) Administrative agencies should only cautiously address problems associated with excessive competition through minimum price regulation.

(C) Administrative agencies often should address problems associated with the adequacy of information available to consumers through a variety of means.

(D) Administrative agencies must have an economic or "efficiency-based" justification for regulation.

1.6. Regarding an agency's rule making authority, which of the following is an accurate statement?

(A) Any agency empowered by Congress to promulgate substantive rules implementing a regulatory scheme adopted by Congress has a concurrent power to promulgate interpretive rules.

(B) Any agency empowered by Congress to enforce a regulatory scheme adopted by Congress has a concurrent power to promulgate substantive rules.

(C) Any grant by Congress to an agency of the power to promulgate substantive rules implementing a regulatory scheme adopted by Congress forecloses challenging the agency's rules on the basis of the statutory authority for the rule.

(D) Any grant by Congress to an agency of the power to promulgate substantive rules implementing a regulatory scheme adopted by Congress forecloses challenging the agency's rules on the basis of the constitutionality of the rule.

1.7. Regarding an agency's authority generally, which of the following is an accurate statement?

(A) If an agency is granted both rule making and adjudicatory authority, the agency must announce new principles prospectively through rule making because making new law through adjudication is inherently unfair and a violation of due process.

(B) If an agency is granted both rule making and adjudicatory authority, the agency generally should announce new principles prospectively through rule making, but mayproceed on a case-by-case basis if it is addressing an emerging regulatory problem arising from variable industry practices.

(C) If an agency is granted both rulemaking and adjudicatory authority, the agency is free to use adjudication to announce new principles and an agency order imposing substantial penalties will not be set aside on the basis of unfair surprise to a regulated person or entity.

(D) If an agency is granted both rulemaking and adjudicatory authority, the agency is free to use adjudication to announce new principles and an agency order imposing a penalty will not be set aside on the basis of substantial reliance by a regulated person or entity on the agency's prior practice.

1.8. Regarding an agency's investigatory powers, which of the following is NOT an accurate statement?

(A) Agencies may issue subpoenas to compel the production of documents or the testimony of persons with relevant information.

(B) Although agencies may compel regulated entities to produce existing documents, they cannot compel regulated entities to create and submit compilations of information that would not otherwise exist.

(C) Agencies may conduct inspections to determine if a regulated entity is in compliance with the law.

(D) None of the above.

1.9. Regarding the ways in which an agency keeps the public informed about its actions, which of the following is an accurate statement?

(A) The Federal Register, which is published by the federal government on a weekly basis, is used by agencies to notify the public regarding proposed and final rules and information about other agency actions.

(B) Each year, agencies publish new regulations promulgated within the previous twelve months in the Code of Federal Regulations.

(C) Agencies must maintain up-to-date indexes regarding, and make available for public inspection and copying, final opinions and other orders made in the adjudication of cases.

(D) Agencies may establish a schedule of fees for the processing of requests for inspection and copying, and must consistently adhere to the applicable fee schedule for such requests.

Rulemaking Procedures: Initiating Rule Making

2.1. Assume that the snowmobiling industry wants the National Park Service to modify a rule pertaining to use of snowmobiles in national parks. Which of the following is the least effective method for prompting the agency to act?

(A) Notifying and educating the agency about the burden the current rule imposes on the industry and thus the need for a modification of the rule.

(B) Notifying the media and getting them to spotlight the plight of the industry and he limited impact that a modification of the rule would have on the parks.

(C) Lobbying congressional representatives and educating them about the plight of the industry and the limited impact that a modification of the rule would have on the parks.

(D) Educating the agency about the plight of the industry and the limited impact that a modification of the rule would have on the parks and, concurrently, filing a formal, written petition asking the agency to begin a rulemaking proceeding.

2.2. Assume that a judicial action has been filed, asking a court to review an agency's failure to act on a § 553(e) petition for rulemaking. According to the petition, Congress man-dated the agency to formulate and make the requested rules within an 18 month timetable. Yet, 24 months have passed and the agency has not even published the requisite notice of rulemaking. Discuss the effect of the statutory timetable on the court's analysis of whether to compel agency rulemaking.

ANSWER:

2.3. Explain the likely remedy that would be imposed by a court which agreed that an agency had unreasonably delayed its compliance with a statutory mandate to formulate and promulgate certain rules.

ANSWER:

Exemptions from APA Notice & Comment Procedures

2.4. Regarding the process of rulemaking, which of the following is an accurate statement?

(A) Notice of the agency's intent to promulgate a rule must be published in the Federal Register.

(B) Notice of the agency's intent to promulgate a rule must be published in the Federal Register, unless the agency statement will constitute an interpretation of a statute or a statement of agency policy.

(C) Notice of the agency's intent to promulgate a rule must be published in the Federal Register, unless the agency statement will constitute an interpretation of the law, a statement of agency policy, or a rule relating to internal agency procedure or practice.

(D) None of the above.

2.5. Discuss the difference between the exemptions in § 553(a) and § 553(b).

ANSWER:

2.6. Which of the following would be least likely to fall within a section 553(b) exception to notice and comment rulemaking procedures?

(A) The Department of Agriculture issued a ban on exportation of fruit from California after declaring an emergency when a Department inspector found a devastating Oriental fruit fly in a trapping device in San Diego, CA.

(B) The U.S. Coast Guard issued a rule establishing a temporary safety zone following a massive oil spill off the coast of Florida.

(C) The Department of Health and Human Services issued a series of rules detailing when health care providers may release personal health care information. The rules were issued without notice and comment because Congress directed the Department to issue the rules within two years and that statutory deadline could not be met if notice and comment procedures were used.

(D) The Department of Labor issued a series of rules detailing how the Occupational Safety and Health Administration (OSHA) should determine which employers to inspect, and when and how to conduct those inspections.

The Toxic Substances Control Act forbids the manufacture, processing, or use of any polychlorinated biphenyls ("PCBs"). However, the Act also authorizes the EPA Administrator to waive the prohibition by rule if it would not present an unreasonable risk of injury to health or the environment. Assume that in 1999, after notice and extensive commentary by interested persons, EPA promulgated a rule relating to use of surfaces contaminated by PCB spills. Under that policy, concrete surfaces could be used after a spill of regulated, liquid PCB (>=50 ppm); however, if the spill resulted in a surface concentration of greater than 10 micrograms of PCBs per 100 square centimeters, extensive cleaning, painting, and marking were required. At that time, EPA explained that the policy would effectively prevent exposure to an unreasonable risk.

Assume further that, in 2001, without notice and comment, EPA amended the rule to eliminate the triggering threshold of surface concentration of greater than 10 micrograms of PCBs per 100 square centimeters; thereby requiring the cleaning, painting and marking for any spill of a regulated, liquid PCB. EPA incorporated in the new rule a statement explaining that good cause existed to forego notice and comment procedures.

> 2.7. If the EPA amendment is challenged for failure to follow notice and comment procedures, which of the following represents the most sound judicial response to EPA's invocation of the good cause exemption?
>
>> (A) The amendment would be set aside because the circumstances did not fall within the scope of the good cause exception to notice and comment.
>>
>> (B) The amendment would not be set aside because notice and comment procedures would have been impracticable, given that PCB spills pose an unreasonable risk of injury to health and the environment.
>>
>> (C) The amendment would not be set aside because notice and comment were unnecessary, given that the amendment contains only minor, routine clarifications that will not have a significant effect on the industry or the public.
>>
>> (D) The amendment would not be set aside because notice and comment would have been contrary to the public interest.

In recent years, the federal agency known as Centers for Disease Control and Prevention ("the CDC") has become increasing vigilant about the need to rapidly identify the incidence of certain diseases; namely, diseases which might indicate that an act of bioterrorism has occurred. Accordingly, assume that, acting pursuant to its rulemaking authority and using notice and comment procedures, the CDC promulgated a regulation ("Rule 501") which requires physicians to report to the CDC, within ten days, the diagnosis of twenty specific diseases referred to as "potential bioterrorism indicators" ("PBIs"). Rule 501 prescribes that a physician's failure to report could lead to imposition of substantial civil penalties.

One year after promulgation of Rule 501, the CDC issued, without notice and comment, and published in the Federal Register a notice entitled the "PBI Guidelines." For each of the twenty PBIs, the PBI Guidelines establish a set the symptoms which, if identified, warrant testing for the PBIs with specific diagnostic tests also set forth in the PBI Guidelines. The diagnostic tests specified by the Guidelines include some tests beyond those that would otherwise be required by the professional standard of care. The PBI Guidelines state that a knowing failure to use the specified diagnostic tests upon identification of the specified symptoms would violate Rule 501 and justify imposition of the Rule 501 civil penalties.

> 2.8. Assuming that the American Medical Association has challenged the PBI Guidelines as being an invalid legislative rule, what is the most sound judicial response?

(A) The court would set aside the PBI Guidelines because Rule 501 provides an inadequate legislative basis for agency enforcement of a duty to use the diagnostic tests specified in the PBI Guidelines.

(B) The court would set aside the PBI Guidelines because the CDC did not intend the Guidelines to have the force and effect of law.

(C) The court would not set aside the PBI Guidelines because the Guidelines simply state what the CDC thinks Rule 501 means, and only clarifies for physicians their existing duty under Rule 501.

(D) The court would not set aside the PBI Guidelines because the CDC published the Guidelines in the Federal Register.

Since 1937, the statute controlling marijuana has excluded the oil and sterilized seed of hemp from the definition of marijuana. Tetrahydrocannabinols ("THC"), the active agent in marijuana, is found in only trace amounts in hemp seeds and oil. Relying on this exemption, U.S. manufacturers have produced and sold consumable products containing sterilized hemp seeds and oil. However, without using notice and comment procedures, the Drug Enforcement Administration (DEA) issued in 2001 a rule which bans all naturally-occurring THC, including that found in hemp seed and oil. Because the 2001 rule bans the sale of consumable products containing hemp oil, cake, or seed, affected manufacturers challenged the rule as being an invalid legislative rule. (Assume no issue exists regarding the DEA's statutory authority to ban all THC, including all naturally-occurring THC, even that found in hemp seed and oil, notwithstanding the 1937 Act's definition of marijuana.) The DEA has argued that the rule is interpretive and exempt from notice and comment; however, the rule is inconsistent with a rule previously promulgated. Specifically, by 1968 THC was being produced synthetically and DEA issued a legislative rule banning "synthetic equivalents" of THC. In 1975, The Acting Administrator of the DEA published a notice in the Federal Register (in response to certain pending litigation) which expressly interpreted the 1968 rule as not covering sterilized hemp seeds or the trace amounts of THC in sterilized seeds and oil.

2.9. Which of the following is the most sound judicial response to the manufacturer's challenge?

(A) The 2001 rule will not be set aside. Because the 1975 notice was merely an interpretation, it can be amended by a non-legislative rule.

(B) The 2001 rule will be set aside. Even if the 1975 notice was merely an interpretation, notice and comment procedures are required to change an agency's interpretation of a legislative regulation if the prior interpretation is sufficiently authoritative and a significant reliance interest is involved.

(C) The 2001 rule will be set aside. Because the 2001 rule is plainly inconsistent with the 1968 rule which regulates only synthetic THC, it cannot be deemed a mere interpretation.

(D) Both (B) and (C) reflect likely judicial responses.

2.10. Explain the rationale underlying the doctrine developed by the United States Circuit Court for the District of Columbia, pursuant to which notice and comment may be required for an interpretative rule providing an interpretation of a legislative or substantive regulation — as opposed to an interpretive rule providing an interpretation of a statute.

ANSWER:

Notice and Comment Procedures

Assume that the Internal Revenue Service decided to update its rules governing what it calls the Flexible Spending Account program. Through this program, employees may set aside and use pretax earnings for certain qualified expenses. Assume that, previously, the IRS permitted pre-tax earnings to be used for only limited health care expenses; and that, in the Notice of Proposed Rulemaking, the IRS explained it wanted to expand the program to include expenditures for many over-the-counter health care items. However, the IRS explained that it intended to exclude expenses for herbal supplements, given concerns over safety and efficacy. Assume that, during the comment period, dozens of consumer advocacy groups submitted information and testimonials supporting inclusion of certain very popular, and safe, herbal weight loss supplements.

Assume that, after the sixty-day comment period and shortly before the IRS issued the Final Rule, representatives of two prominent pharmaceutical companies met with IRS officials and presented evidence showing various risks associated with the herbal weight loss supplements.

2.11. Regarding this meeting, which of the following is a correct statement?

(A) The APA does not expressly prohibit, nor impose limitations on, such communications. However, the IRS should consider putting a summary of the communication in the public record to ensure fairness.

(B) The APA does not expressly prohibit, nor impose limitations on, such communications; thus, the IRS may freely communicate with industry lobbyists without including information about the communications in the public record.

(C) The APA prohibits post-comment communications from interested persons in informal rulemaking, unless a summary of the communication is put in the public record.

(D) The post-comment communication was impermissible because the rulemaking at issue involved competing claims to a valuable privilege.

Assume that, in the Final Rule, the IRS reversed its previously stated position and allowed expenses for certain, specified herbal weight loss supplements. The IRS explained that many comments noted the value and safety of certain herbal weight loss supplements. Pharmaceutical companies challenged the Final Rule, arguing that the IRS's Notice of Proposed Rulemaking did not comply with § 553's requirements.

2.12. Which of the following is the most sound judicial response?

(A) The Final Rule should not be set aside because the notice of proposed rulemaking informed interested parties of the issues to be addressed.

(B) The Final Rule should not be set aside because § 553's notice requirement does not apply to rules relating to public benefits.

(C) The Final Rule should be set aside because it deviates drastically from the notice of proposed rulemaking.

(D) The Final Rule should be set aside because a complete reversal in the agency's position cannot constitute a logical outgrowth of the original proposed rule.

2.13. Explain why non-legislative rules are sometimes referred to as publication rules.

ANSWER:

2.14. Explain why the "concise general statement of basis and purpose" required by § 553(c) is often a complex and detailed explanation of the rationale underlying an agency rule.

ANSWER:

Challenging a Legislative Interpretative Rule

2.15. Describe what is meant by the phrase "legislative rule" and by the phrase "non-legislative rule."

ANSWER:

2.16. Discuss advantages and disadvantages of an agency's choice to use a non-legislative rule; and why an agency may nonetheless elect to use notice and comment for an interpretive rule.

ANSWER:

Under the Social Security Act, the Social Security Administration (SSA) is authorized to pay disability insurance benefits to persons who have a disability. The Act defines disability as follows:

> An individual shall be determined to be under a disability only if his physical or mental impairments are of such severity that he is not only unable to do his previous work but cannot, considering his age, education, and work experience, engage in any other kind of substantial gainful work which exists in the national economy.

SSA denied disability benefits to Tom, who has hypertension and cardiac arrhythmia. Tom applied for benefits after his job as an elevator operator was eliminated. Although recognizing that Tom had a qualifying impairment, the ALJ applied SSA's interpretation as specified in its regulations and rejected Tom's argument that he was disabled because his previous work no longer exists in significant numbers in the national economy.

The district court upheld the SSA determination. According to the court, the grammatical "rule of last antecedent" dictates that a limiting clause or phrase (here, the relative clause "which exists in the national economy") should ordinarily be read as modifying only the noun or phrase that it immediately follows (here, "any other kind of substantial gainful employment"). Thus, the SSA's interpretation of the Act's definition of disability was reasonable.

The Court of Appeals reversed, explaining that, by referring first to "previous work" and then to "any other kind of substantial gainful work which exists in the national economy," the statute unambiguously indicates that the former is a species of the latter. That is, when a sentence sets out one or more specific items followed by "any other" and a description, the specific item(s) must fall within the description. Thus, according to the court, Tom qualified for benefits.

2.17. Assuming the Supreme Court agrees to hear an appeal, which of the following is the most accurate statement?

   (A)   The Supreme Court would likely decline to defer to SSA's interpretation because the APA commands courts to decide all relevant questions of law.

   (B)   The Supreme Court would likely resolve the issue in step-one of the *Chevron v. Natural Resources Defense Council, Inc.*, 467 U.S. 837 (U.S. 1984), analysis because, using traditional tools of statutory interpretation, the Court would find clear congressional intent regarding the precise issue.

   (C)   The Supreme Court would likely resolve the issue in step-two of the *Chevron v. Natural Resources Defense Council, Inc.*, 467 U.S. 837 (U.S. 1984), analysis because Congress was silent on the precise issue at hand.

   (D)   The Supreme Court would likely accord *Chevron v. Natural Resources Defense Council, Inc.*, 467 U.S. 837 (U.S. 1984), deference to the SSA interpretation because the Act's definition of disability is ambiguous.

2.18. Regarding *Chevron v. Natural Resources Defense Council, Inc.*, 467 U.S. 837 (U.S. 1984), deference to agency interpretations of the law, which of the following is an accurate statement?

   (A)   Under *Chevron v. Natural Resources Defense Council, Inc.*, 467 U.S. (U.S. 1984), courts should cede the right to engage in the judicial task of interpreting statutory language whenever the language is susceptible of more than one interpretation.

   (B)   Under *Chevron v. Natural Resources Defense Council, Inc.*, 467 U.S. (U.S. 1984), courts should cede the right to engage in the judicial task of interpreting a statute whenever it appears that Congress intended to leave a gap for the agency to fill relating to a congressionally created program.

(C)   Under *Chevron v. Natural Resources Defense Council, Inc.*, 467 U.S. 837 (U.S. 1984), courts should cede the right to engage in the judicial task of interpreting ambiguous statutory language whenever the task involves reconciling conflicting policies or depends on more than ordinary knowledge respecting matters delegated to agency expertise.

(D)   Under *Chevron v. Natural Resources Defense Council, Inc.*, 467 U.S. 837 (U.S. 1984), courts should never cede the right to engage in the judicial task of interpreting statutory language because to do so would be inconsistent with the institutional function of the federal judiciary.

2.19.   Discuss whether an agency is more likely to prevail in a challenge to a legislative rule interpreting a statute at step-one or step-two of the *Chevron v. Natural Resources Defense Council, Inc.*, 467 U.S. 837 (U.S. 1984), analysis.

ANSWER:

2.20   Explain how the Supreme Court's decisions in *United States v. Mead Corp.*, 533 U.S. 218 (2001) and *Gonzales v. Oregon*, 546 U.S. 243 (2006), clarified the instances in which *Chevron* deference is due to agency interpretations.

ANSWER:

Challenging the Substantive Aspects of a Non-Interpretive Rule

Assume that the Internal Revenue Service decided to update its rules governing what it calls the Flexible Spending Account program. Through this program, employees may set aside and use pretax earnings for certain qualified expenses. Assume that, previously, the IRS permitted pre-tax earnings to be used for only limited health care expenses; but that, in its Notice of Proposed Rulemaking, the IRS explained that it wanted to expand the program to include expenditures for many over-the-counter health care items. However, the IRS explained that it intended to exclude expenses for herbal supplements and treatments, given concerns over safety and efficacy. Assume that, during the comment period, dozens of consumer advocacy groups submitted information and testimonials supporting inclusion of certain very popular, and safe, herbal supplements and treatments; and that, after the sixty-day comment period, and shortly before the IRS issued the Final Rule, representatives of two prominent pharmaceutical companies met with IRS officials and presented evidence showing various risks associated with the herbal supplements and treatments.

Assume that in the Final Rule, the IRS reversed its previously stated position and allowed expenses for certain, specified herbal supplements. The IRS explained that many consumers commented on the value and safety of certain herbal supplements and treatments for a multitude of health related conditions; and herbal manufacturers provided several reports opining to their safety. Further, the IRS noted that its statutory obligation with respect to the Flexible Spending Account program required it to focus primarily on whether it was fair and reasonable, from a tax perspective, to allow certain health-care related expenditures to be paid with pre-tax dollars; and not on the safety and efficacy of available health-care items.

Since the new rules allow pre-tax dollars to be used for non-herbal over-the-counter first aid items/remedies, the IRS concluded that, in light of the evidence of reasonable safety, it was only fair and reasonable to also allow pre-tax dollars to be used for herbal supplements and treatments which are also generally available over-the-counter. In both instances, taxpayers are using income to address health conditions.

2.21. Assuming that the pharmaceutical companies challenge the substantive aspects of the IRS's Final Rule, which of the following statements represents a sound judicial response?

(A) The court would be justified in setting aside the Final Rule if the finding of value and safety of herbal supplements and treatments is unsupported by substantial evidence in the record.

(B) Under the arbitrary and capricious standard, the court would be justified in deferring to the IRS because the Final Rule represents a plausible policy decision.

(C) The court would be justified in deferring to the IRS because the statement of basis and purpose published in the Federal Register demonstrates that the IRS did not improperly consider factors such as safety and efficacy of herbal supplements, and primarily considered fairness and reasonableness.

(D) The court would be justified in setting aside the Final Rule because, in the statement of basis and purpose published in the Federal Register, the IRS failed to adequately explain why herbal supplements and treatments should be treated the same as over-the-counter non-herbal first-aid items/remedies, given legitimate safety and efficacy concerns.

Now assume that the statute authorizing the IRS to promulgate rules implementing the Flexible Spending Account program provides that, upon a petition seeking judicial review of such IRS rules, the federal district courts shall have jurisdiction and shall set aside and hold unlawful a rule on any ground specified in § 706(2) of the APA, or if the court finds that the IRS action is not supported by substantial evidence in the rulemaking record taken as a whole.

2.22. Assuming that the pharmaceutical companies challenge the Final Rule, which of the following statements represents a sound judicial response?

(A) The court would be justified in setting aside the Final Rule if the finding of value and safety of many herbal supplements and treatments is unsupported by substantial evidence in the record.

(B) The court would be justified in deferring to the IRS because the statement of basis and purpose published in the *Federal Register* demonstrates that the IRS did not improperly consider factors such as safety and efficacy of herbal supplements.

(C) The court would be justified in setting aside the Final Rule because, in the statement of basis and purpose published in the *Federal Register*, the IRS failed to adequately explain why herbal supplements and treatments should be treated the same as over-the-counter non-herbal first-aid items/remedies, given legitimate safety and efficacy concerns.

(D) Both (A) and (B) represent sound judicial responses.

2.23. APA § 706 sets forth various reasons why courts may set aside agency rules, in judicial actions in which agency rules are challenged. Describe when the standard of review used by the court in such actions is NOT deferential.

ANSWER:

2.24. In comparing *Chevron v. Natural Resources Defense Council, Inc.*, 467 U.S. 837 (U.S. 1984), review of agency action and "hard look" review of agency action, which of the following is an accurate statement?

(A) Review under step-two of *Chevron v. Natural Resources Defense Council, Inc.*, 467 U.S. 837 (U.S. 1984), is more deferential to the agency than is a "hard look" review.

(B) Both constitute, in essence, de novo review.

(C) "Hard look" review is more deferential to the agency than is review under step-two of *Chevron v. Natural Resources Defense Council, Inc.*, 467 U.S. 837 (U.S. 1984).

(D) In both instances, the reviewing court engages in virtually identical analyses.

2.25. Which of the following is not a valid concern relating to "hard look" judicial review of agency action?

(A) Hard look review is problematic because it allows a reviewing court to inject biases.

(B) Hard look review is problematic because it is inconsistent with the Supreme Court's directive in *Vermont Yankee Nuclear Power Corp. v. Natural Resources Defense Council*, 435 U.S. 579 (1978), that the judiciary may not impose on agencies in a rulemaking proceeding procedural requirements beyond those imposed by Congress.

(C) Hard look review is problematic because it allows a reviewing court to impose a heightened evidentiary standard to factual findings.

(D) Hard look review is problematic because agencies feel compelled to provide contemporaneous explanations of rules beyond what is required by the APA.

2.26. What remedy may a court impose if it determines that an agency, when engaging in rule making, has relied on factors which Congress did not intend for the agency to consider;

or if the agency has failed to articulate a satisfactory explanation for its final rule?

ANSWER:

Beyond the APA: Other Mandated Procedural Requirements for Rulemaking

2.27. Regarding the Regulatory Flexibility Act, which of the following is an accurate statement?

(A) The primary purpose of the Act is to avoid unnecessary federal record keeping and reporting requirements.

(B) The primary purpose of the Act is to compel federal agencies to carefully consider the cost and benefit of additional regulations.

(C) The primary purpose of the Act is to compel federal agencies to carefully consider the potential impact of additional regulations on small businesses.

(D) The primary purpose of the Act is to compel federal agencies to carefully consider the cost imposed on states through new, or amendments to existing, regulatory programs.

2.28. Regarding the Regulatory Flexibility Act, which of the following is an accurate statement?

(A) The Act authorizes courts to review claims of agency noncompliance; and, if found, authorizes courts to remand the rule or to defer enforcement of the rule.

(B) The Act authorizes courts to review claims of agency noncompliance; and, if found, requires courts to remand the rule to the agency and order the Regulatory Flexibility Analysis.

(C) The Act does not allow judicial review of the substance of the Regulatory Flexibility Analysis.

(D) The Act does not create any mechanism for judicial enforcement of the Act's requirement of a Regulatory Flexibility Analysis.

2.29. Regarding Executive Order 12,866, which of the following is an accurate statement?

(A) The Order authorizes courts to review claims of agency noncompliance; and, if found, authorizes courts to remand the rule or to defer enforcement of the rule.

(B) The Order authorizes courts to review claims of agency noncompliance; and, if found, requires courts to remand the rule to the agency and order the required cost/benefit analysis.

(C)   The Order allows judicial review of the substance of an agency's cost/benefit assessment.

(D)   The Order does not create any mechanism for judicial enforcement of the Order's requirement of a cost/benefit assessment.

2.30. Given the many additional sources of mandates (e.g., Executive Orders, the Regulatory Flexibility Act, the Unfunded Mandates Reform Act, and the Paperwork Reduction Action), explain whether the additional procedural requirements enhance or impede administrative regulation.

ANSWER:

2.31. Regarding negotiated rulemaking, which of the following is an accurate statement?

(A)   Executive Order 12,866 requires agencies to use negotiated rulemaking if at all feasible.

(B)   Whether an agency uses negotiated rulemaking is determined by the agency without input from persons with interests likely to be affected by the rulemaking.

(C)   If an agency decides to use negotiated rulemaking, the agency must establish a negotiated rulemaking committee and the committee must consider the matter proposed and attempt to reach a consensus regarding the matter proposed.

(D)   If a properly established negotiated rulemaking committee reaches consensus on the matter proposed, the agency may publish in the Federal Register the committee's conclusions as a final rule.

3.1. Describe the key difference(s) between agency rulemaking and agency adjudication.

ANSWER:

3.2. Agency adjudication is sometimes referred to as "quasi-judicial," since the resulting "order" is somewhat akin to a judgment imposed by a court. However, many agency adjudications look nothing like a judicial proceeding. Discuss why an agency adjudication may properly lack many of the trappings of judicial proceedings.

ANSWER:

The Clean Water Act (CWA) prohibits the discharge of any pollutant into navigable waters unless the point source operator has obtained an EPA permit. However, the CWA also authorizes the EPA to issue exemptions in appropriate cases. Under the CWA, a point source operator is entitled to an exemption if, "after opportunity for public hearing," the operator can demonstrate to the satisfaction of the Administrator that all statutory requirements for the exemption are satisfied. The Big O Company applied for and was granted an exemption allowing the discharge of materials in the river adjacent to Big O's property. Shortly thereafter a regional antipollution group challenged, via judicial review, the EPA decision to grant the exemption. One argument made by the group is that procedures used by the EPA contravened APA adjudication requirements. The EPA responded that the APA protections did not apply.

3.3. Which of the following statements reflects the most sound judicial response?

(A) The EPA will likely win on this issue because the Supreme Court has held that APA's adjudication procedures apply only if Congress expressly requires that the determination is to be made "on the record" after opportunity for an agency hearing.

(B) It is unclear which side will likely win on this issue because the reviewing court will construe the statute as a whole to determine whether Congress intended to require the APA adjudication requirements.

(C) The antipollution group will likely win on this issue because a presumption exists that APA procedures apply whenever Congress imposes a "hearing" requirement unless Congress clearly indicates otherwise.

(D) The EPA will likely win on this issue because the reviewing court will always defer to the agency determination of the issue.

Medicare Part B covers physician and outpatient hospital services, including diagnostic tests, laboratory services, durable medical equipment, and many other specialized services for persons eligible to participate in the Medicare program. However, the program will not cover services which are not reasonable and necessary for the diagnosis or treatment of illness or injury. Claims for reimbursement are submitted to entities under contract with the Centers for Medicare and Medicaid (CMM). The contractors make initial determinations of whether reimbursement is proper. If the claim is denied, the Medicare beneficiary may seek, from the contractor, a reconsideration on the written record. If the denial is affirmed and the claim is over $500, the claimant may appeal the decision to an ALJ. The ALJ presides over an oral, evidentiary hearing and makes a determination. Claimants can appeal the ALJ decision to an Appeals Council, whose decision is deemed the final agency decision. If the claim is over $1000, a Medicare beneficiary may seek judicial review of final determinations.

Under the statute, the reviewing ALJ has power to enter, upon the pleadings and transcript of the record, a judgment affirming, modifying, or reversing the CMM decision, with or without remanding the cause for a rehearing. However, the findings of the CMM as to any fact, if supported by substantial evidence, shall be conclusive. Assume that the Supreme Court has held that Congress intended that the APA's formal adjudication procedures apply from the point of the ALJ hearing.

Assume that Tony, a participant in the Medicare program, was diagnosed with prostate cancer and opted for a treatment called cryosurgical ablation. After the surgery, Tony requested payment from Medicare in the amount of $10,000 to cover physician and outpatient expenses. Medicare denied payment, stating that the service was considered experimental and thus not reasonable and necessary. Upon reconsideration, the denial was affirmed and Tony has requested an ALJ hearing.

3.4. Regarding the ALJ hearing, which of the following is an accurate statement?

(A) The decision of the ALJ may be based in part on facts or information concerning the mortality rate of cryosurgical ablation, even if that information lacks sufficient evidence in the record, as long as Tony is provided a reasonable opportunity to present any contrary evidence he may have.

(B) In order to affirm the denial of benefits, the ALJ will need to find that the preponderance of the evidence supports the contractor's initial denial.

(C) The decision of the ALJ will constitute a recommendation to the agency.

(D) Tony cannot be precluded from presenting his case through the oral testimony of local oncologists.

3.5. Regarding the ALJ hearing, which of the following is an accurate statement?

(A) If the agency, CMM, has issued guidance to all contractors explaining its official position that cryosurgical ablation is experimental, the ALJ cannot issue an order in favor of Tony.

(B) If the agency, CMM, has issued guidance to all contractors explaining its official position that cryosurgical ablation is experimental, the ALJ may nonetheless issue an order in favor of Tony if Tony presents a preponderance of the evidence showing that the CMM position is unwarranted.

(C) Assuming no official agency position and that Tony presents his argument through the oral testimony of local oncologists, the ALJ cannot properly issue an order against Tony if the only contrary evidence in the record consists of affidavits of other equally qualified oncologists.

(D) None of the above.

3.6. Regarding the appeal to the Appeals Council, which of the following is an accurate statement?

(A) The Appeals Council can set aside the decision of the ALJ only if it is unsupported by substantial evidence in the record.

(B) The Appeals Council can set aside the decision of the ALJ only if it is arbitrary, capricious, or an abuse of discretion.

(C) The Appeals Council may conduct a de novo review of the matter, including presiding over the taking of evidence.

(D) The Appeals Council may conduct a de novo review of the matter, but will limit its review to the § 556(e) record complied by the ALJ and to the written submissions allowed by the APA.

3.7. Assuming that the ALJ and the Appeals Council issue decisions affirming the initial denial of Tony's claim for reimbursement, which of the following is an accurate statement relating to judicial review?

(A) If unsupported by substantial evidence in the record, the court is authorized only to set aside the CMM order.

(B) The court may modify or reverse the decision of the agency, with or without remanding the cause for a rehearing, upon a finding that the agency findings of fact were arbitrary and capricious.

(C) The court may modify or reverse the decision of the agency, with or without remanding the cause for a rehearing, when appropriate.

(D) None of the above.

Now assume that Jane, who also participates in the Medicare program, has been diagnosed with stage III breast cancer. Her physician recommended an expensive treatment involving high dose chemotherapy and a bone marrow transplant (HDC/BMT). Jane agreed to the treatment and has submitted a claim to Medicare for reimbursement of the expenses incurred as a result of the HDC/BMT. The Medicare contractor denied payment, stating that HDC/BMT was considered experimental. Upon reconsideration, the denial was affirmed; and the ALJ affirmed the denial. Jane has appealed the denial to the Appeals Council. While Jane's appeal is pending, the Administrator of CMM sent a memorandum to the persons serving on the Appeals Council. In the memorandum, the Administrator noted her concern about Medicare being obligated to cover HDC/BMT for women with breast cancer, given the high cost of the treatment and the high prevalence of breast cancer in the Medicare population; and urged the members of the Appeals Council to move cautiously.

3.8. Regarding the Administrator's memorandum, which of the following is an accurate statement?

(A) The memorandum constitutes a permissible communication and the Appeals Council is not required to make the memorandum part of the public record.

(B) The memorandum constitutes a permissible communication, but the Appeals Council must still make the memorandum part of the public record.

(C) The memorandum constitutes an impermissible ex parte communication which must be disregarded by the Appeals Council.

(D) The memorandum constitutes an impermissible ex parte communication, but it does not need to be disregarded as long as it is made a part of the public record.

Assume now that the Administrator attached to her memorandum a letter addressed to the agency and signed by the presidents/CEOs of a number of the nation's largest health insurance providers. The letter explains to the Administrator that private insurers have determined that HDC/BMT for women with stage III breast cancer is experimental treatment and thus excluded from coverage under most private health insurance policies.

3.9. Regarding this communication, which of the following is an accurate statement?

(A) The memorandum and letter constitute a permissible communication and the Appeals Council is not required to make the memorandum or the letter part of the public record.

(B) The attached letter constitutes an impermissible ex parte communication which must be disregarded by the Appeals Council.

(C) The attached letter constitutes an impermissible ex parte communication, but it does not need to be disregarded as long as it is made a part of the public record.

(D) None of the above.

Assume that the Appeals Council affirmed the ALJ's denial of Jane's claim for Medicare reimbursement for the expenses incurred as a result of the HDC/BMT, agreeing that the treatment was experimental and thus not reasonable and necessary. Jane learned of the letter sent to CMM by the private insurers only after the Appeals Council issued its order because the letter had not been made a part of the public record. Jane has filed a suit for judicial review, asking the court to set aside the CMM decision as a consequence of the impermissible ex parte communication.

CMM has argued that reversal is not necessary or appropriate because each member of the Appeals Council has stated under oath that he or she was not influenced by the letter.

3.10. Which of the following is the most sound judicial response?

(A) Although the letter constitutes an impermissible ex parte communication, the court need not reverse or set aside the CMM order because it is not clear that the agency decision making process was irrevocably tainted.

(B) The attached letter constitutes an impermissible ex parte communication and, because the APA was violated, the court must set aside the CMM order.

(C) The attached letter constitutes an impermissible ex parte communication and the court must set aside the CMM order because it is clear that the decision making process was irrevocably tainted since the letter was not made part of the public record.

(D) None of the above.

Assume that an inspector from the Occupational Safety and Health Administration (OSHA) issued a citation against United Motors for a number of substantial workplace safety violations at its Motortown plant. United Motors disputed that it violated any safety standards and requested a hearing before an ALJ. The inspector testified at the hearing as to conditions at United Motors' plant. Two days after the hearing, while preparing his written findings and conclusions, the ALJ telephoned the inspector to discuss further the evidence relating to conditions at United Motors' plant.

3.11. Discuss the appropriateness of the telephone communication between the ALJ and the OSHA inspector.

ANSWER:

3.12. Describe the function of a "presiding employee."

ANSWER:

3.13. Identify five procedures required by the APA for informal adjudications.

ANSWER:

3.14. Discuss the extent to which ALJs (administrative law judges) are independent and neutral when they serve as a presiding officer at an administrative hearing.

ANSWER:

3.15. Explain the scope of review used by an agency when an ALJ's recommended decision is appealed.

ANSWER:

3.16. Regarding due process protections, which of the following is an accurate statement?

   (A) Due process protections are triggered by all adverse agency adjudications.

   (B) Due process protections are triggered by agency rules imposing burdensome costs on regulated businesses.

   (C) Due process protections are almost always triggered by agency adjudications terminating government welfare or social services benefits.

   (D) Due process protections are triggered only by agency adjudications adversely affecting legally recognized rights; and not by agency actions affecting claims to government privileges.

Assume that the State University hired Susan to fill a "visiting professor" position. The position was for a fixed term of one academic year. At the end of the term, Susan was not re-hired. Further, the University did not provide Susan with any notice that she would not be re-hired; and did not provide any reason for the non-retention.

3.17. If Susan challenges the University's decision as constituting a violation of her due process rights, since she was not afforded notice and an opportunity to address any possible concerns about her teaching, which of the following represents the most sound judicial response?

   (A) A court would not set aside the determination because courts lack jurisdiction to review university personnel decisions.

   (B) A court would not set aside the determination because Susan had no legitimate claim of entitlement to retention and the determination did not create any impermissible stigma giving rise to a protected liberty interest.

   (C) A court would set aside the determination because it will interfere with Susan's liberty interest in finding future teaching positions.

   (D) A court would set aside the determination because Susan has been deprived of a property interest.

3.18. Describe when government action creating "stigma" can give rise to a liberty interest worthy of due process protections.

ANSWER:

Assume that New York has enacted a law requiring convicted sex offenders to register with the New York State Department of Public Safety upon their release into the community. Each offender must provide his name, address, photograph and a DNA sample; notify the DPS of any change in residence; and submit an updated photo periodically. The law requires DPS to post the registry on its website and to make the registry available to the public in certain state offices. The registry contains the following statement. "This registry is intended to facilitate access to publicly available information about persons convicted of sexual offenses. It is based on the state's decision that the public has a right to be warned about dangerous persons living in communities within the state."

3.19. Regarding due process rights of convicted sex offenders who may be identified and located through the registry, which of the following is an accurate statement?

(A) Convicted sex offenders have no right to a hearing prior to placing identifying information in the publicly accessible registry because the public has a strong interest in access to this information.

(B) Convicted sex offenders have no right to a hearing prior to placing identifying information in the publicly accessible registry because no dispute exists as to any relevant fact, and thus they have nothing to prove or disprove.

(C) Convicted sex offenders have a strong argument that they have right to a hearing prior to placing identifying information in the publicly accessible registry because placing the information in the registry creates an impermissible stigma without notice and an opportunity to be heard.

(D) Convicted sex offenders have a strong argument that they have right to a hearing prior to placing identifying information in the publicly-accessible registry because placing the information in the registry creates an impermissible stigma without notice and an opportunity to be heard, plus, it adversely impacts their right to privacy and their ability to live in certain communities within the state.

3.20. Regarding the factors a court must consider to determine whether additional procedural protections are warranted by the due process clause, which of the following is the most accurate statement?

(A) Courts must balance the gravity of the deprivation against the financial burden to agencies associated with additional procedural protections.

(B) Courts must balance the risk of erroneous deprivation against the value of additional procedural protections.

(C) Courts must balance the gravity of the deprivation against the risk of error involved using the procedural protections currently used by the agency.

(D) Courts must balance the gravity of the deprivation and the risk of error associated with the procedural protections currently used by the agency, against the burden to agencies which would result from additional procedural protections.

Judicial Review of Agency Adjudications

The Department of Health and Human Services (HHS) regulates the conduct of research for which federal funds are used. Assume that HHS has issued rules which preclude a researcher from participating in the conduct of a clinical trial if the researcher holds a significant financial interest which could be affected by the outcome of the trial, unless the researcher provides to human subjects participating in the trial a full and adequate disclosure of the nature and extent of the financial interest. The disclosure must be made as part of the process of obtaining the human subject's informed consent to participate in the trial. If research is conducted in violation of the HHS rules, HHS may issue a cease and desist order affecting current trials, withhold federal funds from future trials, or prohibit future applications for federal funding. Assume that HHS determined that Dr. Smith had violated the HHS rule by failing to provide an adequate disclosure of her significant financial interest in a drug being tested in a clinical trial for which Dr. Smith is the principle investigator. HHS learned of the violation through complaints provided to HHS from graduate student researchers involved in the clinical trial.

Assume that HHS initiated an enforcement proceeding; and that HHS rules require HHS to follow formal APA hearing procedures. During the agency proceeding, the ALJ found in favor of

Dr. Smith. Dr. Smith testified that she always provided the required disclosure; that it was always adequate because she read a prepared text; and she demonstrated how she provided the disclosure. The ALJ rejected the testimony of HHS's key witness, John, who stated that he was present on several occasions when Dr. Smith purportedly disclosed her financial interest. According to John, Dr. Smith's tone of voice and body language were designed to minimize any concerns a potential subject might have about Dr. Smith's financial interest; and to maximize the subject's trust in Dr. Smith.

The ALJ's written findings and conclusions explained that Dr. Smith was a sincere and credible witness, and that her tone of voice and demeanor would certainly alert a subject to the importance of the information being conveyed. Regarding John, the ALJ explained that he seemed nervous and was unsure of the dates on which he was present during the informed consent process.

HHS appealed the ALJ decision to the Human Research Commission, the appeals division within HHS for this type of proceeding. The Commission reversed the ALJ decision. The findings and conclusions of the Commission explained that, although the content of Dr. Smith's prepared text was adequate, the tone and body language used during disclosure could clearly impact the adequacy of the disclosure, and, as in other similar cases, it was very likely that Smith sought to use a tone engendering trust. Further, the Commission explained that John's testimony should not have been discounted. As a graduate student researcher he had reason to be nervous during the hearing. Further, the Commission noted that there was no reason to suspect John's testimony simply because he was unclear about precise dates, given that graduate student researchers assisting in clinical trials typically are extremely busy and overworked. Dr. Smith has sought judicial review of the HHS determination.

3.21. Regarding the standard of review used by court, which of the following is an accurate statement?

   (A) The court may set aside the HHS determination that Dr. Smith's disclosure was not "full and adequate" if the court finds that the determination is unsupported by substantial evidence in the record.

(B) The court may set aside the HHS determination that Dr. Smith's disclosure was not "full and adequate" if the court finds that the determination was arbitrary and capricious.

(C) The court may set aside the HHS determination that Dr. Smith's disclosure was not "full and adequate" if the court finds that the determination, although having an evidentiary basis in the record, lacks a reasonable basis in law.

(D) All of the above.

3.22. Regarding judicial review, which of the following is an accurate statement?

(A) In reviewing the record, the court will consider the evidence supporting HHS's determination in light of the body of evidence opposed to HHS's view.

(B) In reviewing the record, the court will consider only the evidence supporting HHS's determination.

(C) In reviewing the record, the court will give greater weight to the evidence supporting HHS's determination than to the evidence opposed to HHS's view.

(D) None of the above.

3.23. Regarding Dr. Smith's action for judicial review, which of the following represents the most sound judicial response?

(A) HHS's determination that Dr. Smith's disclosure was not "full and adequate" must be set aside because it rests on testimonial evidence discredited by the ALJ, and the ALJ's credibility inferences were based on witness demeanor.

(B) HHS's determination that Dr. Smith's disclosure was not "full and adequate" need not be set aside because, although the ALJ's credibility inferences were based on witness demeanor, the Commission provided sound reasons, some grounded in experience, for its contrary determination.

(C) HHS's determination that Dr. Smith's disclosure was not "full and adequate" must be set aside because the Commission was bound by the credibility determinations of the ALJ.

(D) In applying the substantial evidence standard of review, the ALJ's credibility determination is not relevant because it is not part of the record for judicial review.

3.24. Assume now that neither Congress nor HHS requires the determination of "full and adequate disclosure" to be made pursuant to formal APA procedures. Regarding judicial review of HHS's determination, which of the following is an accurate statement?

(A) The court may set aside the HHS determination that Dr. Smith's disclosure was not "full and adequate" if the court finds that the determination is unsupported by substantial evidence in the record.

(B) The court may set aside the HHS determination that Dr. Smith's disclosure was not "full and adequate" if the court finds that the determination is arbitrary and capricious.

(C) The court may set aside the HHS determination that Dr. Smith's disclosure was not "full and adequate" if the court finds that the determination, although having an evidentiary basis in the record, lacks a reasonable basis in law.

(D) Both (B) and (C).

3.25. If the HHS proceeding constituted informal adjudication and the HHS rules did not require use of formal APA procedures, which of the following is an accurate statement?

(A) If the Commission did not prepare a contemporaneous explanation of the basis for its findings and conclusions, it would be acceptable for the agency to support its action upon judicial review with affidavits of the Commission members explaining the basis for their decisions.

(B) If the Commission did not prepare a contemporaneous explanation of the basis for its findings and conclusions, the court in an action for judicial review of the action should require the Commission members to give testimony explaining the basis for their decisions.

(C) The Commission likely would prepare a contemporaneous explanation of the basis for its findings and conclusions.

(D) The Commission likely would not prepare a contemporaneous explanation of the basis for their findings and conclusions.

3.26. When a party seeks judicial review of an agency's order, may the court stay the effectiveness of the order during the pendency of the review?

ANSWER:

3.27 Able Time, Inc. imported a shipment of watches into the United States. The watches bore the mark "TOMMY," which is a registered trademark owned by Tommy Hilfiger Licensing, Inc. The Bureau of Customs and Border Protection (Customs) at the Newark airport in New Jersey seized the watches pursuant to the Tariff Act, which authorizes seizure of any "merchandise bearing a counterfeit mark." 19 U.S.C. § 1526(e). Pursuant to the statute, Customs imposed a civil penalty upon Able Time and thereafter filed an *in rem* forfeiture action against the watches in the local federal district court.

In the judicial action, Able Time argues that, because Tommy Hilfiger did not make watches at the time of the seizure, the watches imported by Able Time were not counterfeit, and thus the civil penalty imposed by Customs was unlawful. The government argues that the Tariff Act does not require the owner of the registered mark to make the same type of goods as those bearing the offending mark. The government acknowledges that such a requirement is commonplace in many related trademark statutes but maintains that Congress did not intend to include such a requirement (known as an "identity of goods or services" requirement) in the Tariff Act. Pointing to its generally conferred authority to promulgate substantive regulations, the government argues that the agency's interpretation is entitled to deference under *Chevron*.

The Tariff Act, 19 U.S.C. § 1526(a), provides that: "[I]t shall be unlawful to import into the United States any merchandise of foreign manufacture if such merchandise . . . bears a trademark owned by a citizen of, or by a corporation or association created or organized within, the United States . . . unless written consent of the owner of such trademark is produced."

Assuming that the court finds that Congress in the Tariff Act was silent on the precise issue, which of the following is an accurate statement?

(A) Because the agency is interpreting a statutory provision, the court must find that the agency's view warrants *Chevron* deference.

(B) Because the agency's interpretation of the statutory provision was formulated in the course of routine enforcement action, the agency's view is binding on the court.

(C) Because the agency's interpretation of the statutory provision was formulated in the course of routine enforcement action, the court should defer only if the agency's view reflects thorough consideration, valid reasoning, and consistency with other enforcement actions.

(D) An agency interpretation advanced only in the course of litigation necessarily lacks the power of persuasion necessary to warrant any form of judicial deference.

4.1. Which of the following involves a retroactive law?

(A) Application of a new rule or policy to existing facts.

(B) Application of a new rule to future facts.

(C) Application of a new rule to cases that are based on facts that occur after the law was passed.

(D) All of the above.

4.2. Retroactive laws are particularly objectionable for the following reasons:

(A) Since retroactive laws are announced after the fact (after a regulated entity has engaged in the subject conduct), they deprive regulated entities of advance "notice" regarding the content and meaning of laws.

(B) Since retroactive laws are announced after the fact, they deprive regulated entities of a fair opportunity to bring their conduct into compliance with the law.

(C) Since retroactive laws are announced after the fact, they are less likely to be consistent with due process.

(D) All of the above.

4.3. To the extent that "retroactivity" is precluded by the United States Constitution, the prohibition is imposed under:

(A) The Equal Protection Clause.

(B) The First Amendment.

(C) The Supremacy Clause.

(D) The Due Process Clause.

4.4. Because of the problems presented by retroactive laws, such laws are:

(A) Never constitutional.

(B) Always constitutional.

(C) Sometimes constitutional.

(D) None of the above.

The United States Department of Agriculture (DOA), which administers the Animal Welfare Act, charges Wild West Puppy Breeders (Wild West) of Dothan, Alabama, with violating the rules under which puppies can be shipped. The rules prohibit the shipment of puppies under "inhumane conditions" which the rules define as including shipments during periods of "excessively hot temperatures." The only defense under the statute is that the breeder took adequate steps to mitigate the heat by, for example, providing air conditioning. Wild West shipped puppies during July when the temperature consistently exceeded 90 degrees. Given that Wild West is located in Alabama, and given that summer temperatures usually exceed 90 degrees in Alabama, Wild West argues that 90 degrees should not be regarded as an "excessively hot temperature" in Alabama in July. Wild West notes that its puppies are routinely kept during non-shipment periods in 90 degree heat. You are a legal adviser at the DOA which will hold that Wild West violated the humane treatment rule. However, DOA is concerned about whether it can or should announce its application of the rule in an adjudicative proceeding.

4.5. Please write a short answer advising whether, when administrative agencies issue adju-dicative decisions (in other words, their opinions in litigated administrative cases), those decisions can be applied retroactively.

ANSWER:

The United States Department of Labor (DOL) has decided to issue a new legislative rule using notice and comment procedures. DOL is deeply concerned about the way that regulated entities have been interpreting various provisions of the Occupational Safety and Health Act. Because DOL believes that the new rule was implicit in the existing regulatory scheme, it wants to apply the new rule retroactively. The Secretary has come to you for advice about whether he has the power to apply the new rule retroactively.

4.6. How would you advise the Secretary? Please write a short answer advising whether, when administrative agencies issue legislative rules (e.g., "notice and comment" rules), they may they do so retroactively.

ANSWER:

The Securities and Exchange Commission (SEC) issues a press release that articulates its interpretation of the federal securities laws. Because the press release states an "interpretation" of existing law, the SEC makes it clear that it intends to apply the interpretation to all present and future cases. Norwest Industries is upset by the interpretation insofar as it might apply to pre-existing conduct, and has come to you for advice about whether it is permissible to apply the rule to prior conduct.

4.7. You do some research and determine that, when administrative agencies issue informal policies and statements (e.g., advice or interpretations), those policies and informal statements are:

(A) Never applied retroactively.

(B) Frequently applied retroactively.

(C) Sometimes applied retroactively.

(D) Always applied retroactively.

The United States Department of Energy (DOE) hears a case as part of its adjudicative process. At the end of the proceeding, DOE issues a new "adjudicative rule" designed to govern that adjudicative proceeding as well as future adjudicative proceedings. The defendant in the adjudicative proceeding objects that the new rule should not be applied to its prior conduct.

4.8. Under *National Labor Relations Board v. Bell Aerospace*, 416 U.S. (1974), the determination of whether the new rule can be applied retroactively depends on:

(A) The agency's preference as to whether it wants to apply the rule retroactively or prospectively.

(B) A balancing of the benefits of retroactivity against the "mischief" that retroactive application would produce.

(C) Whether those affected by the retroactive rule would suffer harm.

(D) None of the above.

4.9. *National Labor Relations Board v. Bell Aerospace*, 416 U.S. (1974), benefit-mischief analysis applies to which of the following:

(A) Adjudicative rules, as well as legislative rules and informal agencies policies and interpretations.

(B) Adjudicative rules only.

(C) Legislative and adjudicative rules, but not informal agency policies and interpretations.

(D) Adjudicative rules, as well as informal agency policies and interpretations, but not legislative rules.

4.10. In *Retail, Wholesale and Department Store Union v. National Labor Relations Board*, 466 F. 2d 380 (D.C. Cir. 1972), the court attempted to clarify the *National Labor Relations Board v. Bell Aerospace*, 416 U.S. (1974), mischief analysis. In that case, the court held that which of the following factors (among others) should be considered in determining whether an agency can apply a new adjudicative rule retroactively:

(A) Whether the particular rule is one of first impression.

(B) Whether the new rule represents an abrupt departure from well-established practice or merely attempts to fill a void in an unsettled area of law.

(C) The extent to which the party against whom the new rule is applied relied on the former rule.

(D) All of the above.

Now let's return to our prior example of the United States Department of Agriculture (DOA), the Animal Welfare Act, and Wild West Puppy Breeders. As you may recall, DOA charged Wild West with violating the rules under which puppies can be shipped. The rules prohibit the shipment of puppies under "inhumane conditions" which the rules define as including shipments during periods of "excessively hot temperatures." The only defense under the statute is that the breeder took adequate steps to mitigate the heat by, for example, providing air conditioning. Wild West shipped puppies during July when the temperature consistently exceeded 90 degrees. Given that Wild West is located in Alabama, and given that summer temperatures usually exceed 90 degrees in Alabama, Wild West argues that 90 degrees should not be regarded as an "excessively hot temperature" in Alabama in July. Wild West notes that its puppies are routinely kept during non-shipment periods in 90 degree heat. Suppose that DOA offers proof that it has consistently used 85 degrees as a "cut-off" number for summer shipments. As a result, it has cited numerous companies for shipping puppies in heat exceeding 85 degrees, and has consistently imposed sanctions. In addition DOA has published these decisions.

4.11. Under these circumstances, please write a short answer discussing whether the DOA can apply its interpretation retroactively to Wild West.

ANSWER:

In the prior question, would the result be different if the DOA had not consistently interpreted the humane treatment rule as having an 85 degree cut-off for shipments. On the contrary, just two days before the shipment, Wild West called for advice about whether it was permissible to ship puppies in 90 degree heat. A DOA inspector told Wild West that it was permissible to do so. The inspector went on to state that "Heck, it rarely drops below 90 degrees in Alabama in the summer."

4.12. Please write a short answer discussing whether, under these revised facts, the DOA can apply its interpretation retroactively to Wild West.

ANSWER:

The Securities and Exchange Commission (SEC) issues a press release that articulates its interpretation of the federal securities laws. Because the press release states an "interpretation" of existing law, the SEC makes it clear that it intends to apply the interpretation to all present and future cases. Norwest Industries is upset by the interpretation insofar as it might apply to pre-existing conduct, and has come to you for advice about whether it is permissible to apply the rule to prior conduct.

4.13. Important factors to be considered in determining whether the new interpretation can be applied retroactively are whether:

(A) The interpretation is implicit in existing securities laws, but has never been explicitly articulated.

(B) The interpretation reflects a radical departure from the SEC's prior interpretation of the securities laws.

(C) Whether the SEC likes the regulated entity against which the interpretation is being applied.

(D) Both (A) and (B).

Retail, Wholesale and Department Store Union v. National Labor Relations Board, 466 F. 2d 380 (D.C. Cir. 1972), involved a strike against a soft drink manufacturer. After the strike was settled, the manufacturer refused to hire back employees who were permanently replaced during the strike to fill new job openings. At the time, the NLRB's case law provided that, when an employee was permanently replaced, the employer was under no obligation to rehire him/her. On the contrary, the employer was entitled to treat the replaced employee like any other applicant for employment. Although the employer was not allowed to discriminate against the replaced employee, it was not required to give the employee any preference either. Then, in *National Labor Relations Board v. Fleetwood Trailer Co.*, 389 U.S. 375 (1967), the NLRB changed its rule and held that former strikers were entitled to preference over new hires (although it was not required to displace permanent replacements who were hired during the strike). In *Retail, Wholesale*, the NLRB sought to apply the *Fleetwood* decision even though the manufacturer's conduct took place prior to the NLRB's change of rule. The NLRB ordered the manufacturer to provide reinstatement and back pay to striking employees who were not rehired.

4.14. Please write a short answer indicating whether the NLRB should be allowed to apply the *Fleetwood* decision retroactively to the manufacturer.

ANSWER:

5.1. The term "non-legislative" rule refers to administrative rules that are created:

    (A)   Adjudicatively.

    (B)   Through rulings and interpretations.

    (C)   Any non-legislative means.

    (D)   All of the above.

5.2. As a form of administrative legislation, non-legislative rules are:

    (A)   Frequently used.

    (B)   Never used.

    (C)   Sometimes used.

    (D)   Always used.

5.3. In *SEC v. Chenery Corp.*, 332 U.S. 194 (1947) (*Chenery II*), and other cases, the United States Supreme Court held that administrative agencies should be encouraged to articulate policy legislatively, rather than adjudicatively, because:

    (A)   Agencies that possess rulemaking power have less reason to rely on ad hoc adjudication to formulate new rules of conduct.

    (B)   The function of filling in the interstices of a statute should be performed, as much as possible, through the quasi-legislative promulgation of rules to be applied in the future.

    (C)   Legislative rules are preferable to adjudicative rules because they provide interested parties with notice of proposed changes and an opportunity to provide input.

    (D)   All of the above.

5.4. *Chenery II* also held that:

    (A)   Administrative agencies must use legislative rulemaking procedures whenever possible to the exclusion of non-legislative procedures.

(B)   Administrative agencies have discretion about whether to use legislative or non-legislative procedures.

(C)   Non-legislative procedures should be used only as a last resort.

(D)   None of the above.

5.5.   In *Chenery II*, the Court further held that:

(A)   Any rigid requirement that all rules must be promulgated quasi-legislatively would make the process inflexible and incapable of dealing with many of the specialized problems that arise.

(B)   Not every principle essential to the effective administration of a statute can or should be case immediately into the mold of a general rule.

(C)   Some principles must await their own development, while others must be adjusted to meet particular, unforeseeable, situations.

(D)   All of the above.

5.6.   Which of the following additional propositions were articulated in *Chenery II?* Did the Court say that administrative agencies:

(A)   Simply cannot articulate all rules and policies legislatively.

(B)   Must be free to "fill in the interstices" of regulatory schemes through non-legislative means.

(C)   Have discretion about whether to proceed legislatively or adjudicatively.

(D)   All of the above.

There has been much debate about whether agencies should be allowed to articulate policy adjudicatively, or whether they should be required to do so legislatively. Many commentators argue that legislative procedures are preferable because they allow greater participation in rulemaking processes by those subject to those processes. Nevertheless, many agencies continue to articulate policy by non-legislative means.

5.7.   Please write a short answer indicating why, despite the benefits of legislative procedures, agencies might prefer to articulate policy by non-legislative means.

ANSWER:

5.8.   Adjudicative procedures are arguably a less desirable method for creating rules. As we know, they provide the agency with a lesser range of criticism, advice, and data. Which of the following criticisms of adjudicative rules is INVALID:

(A) Adjudicative procedures frequently produce rules that are applied retroactively.

(B) Adjudicative procedures often single out a one regulated entity for regulatory action.

(C) Adjudicative procedures cannot be used to create bright line rules.

(D) None of the above.

5.9. Some administrative agencies prefer to create rules adjudicatively. Which of the following reasons is NOT likely to motivate an agency to use adjudicative procedures?

(A) An agency may wish to insulate its processes from political pressures.

(B) An agency, by proceeding against a single entity in an adjudicative proceeding, is likely to be able to proceed more quickly and less expensively.

(C) If an agency chooses to proceed by adjudication, it can choose its defendant.

(D) None of the above.

5.10. Historically, "legislative rules" (rules created through informal or formal rulemaking processes) have been treated as "binding" and as having the "force and effect of law." As a result, those subject to validly promulgated legislative rules were required to respect and follow them. By contrast, are non-legislative rules binding? Please write a short answer discussing this issue.

ANSWER:

5.11. The weight given to a non-legislative rule depends on:

(A) The format in which it is issued since some courts treat non-legislative rules issued in some formats more respectfully than they treat non-legislative rules issued in other formats.

(B) The whim of the reviewing court.

(C) The status of the official issuing the non-legislative rule.

(D) All of the above.

5.12. An administrative agency issues a non-legislative rule interpreting a regulatory scheme.

Later, the agency changes its mind regarding the content of the rule. Please write a short answer indicating whether the agency may change its non-legislative rule and the manner by which it must do so.

ANSWER:

5.13. In *National Labor Relations Board v. Wyman-Gordon Co.*, 394 U.S. 759 (1969), the Court held that:

(A) Agencies may not articulate rules adjudicatively and apply them purely prospectively.

(B) In adjudicative proceedings, agencies may use hybrid procedures in which they invite interested parties to submit comments.

(C) In adjudicative proceedings, agencies may never articulate "rules."

(D) None of the above.

5.14. Which of the following statements is correct?

(A) A non-legislative rule is an oxymoron (since rules, by definition, must be created legislatively) and therefore invalid.

(B) Non-legislative rules are frequently used by administrative agencies to articulate new policies.

(C) Non-legislative procedures can only be used in emergency situations.

(D) All of the above.

5.15. Which of the following statements is correct?

(A) Although agencies are free to create non-legislative rules, they must allow the public to have input regarding the content of those rules.

(B) Although agencies are free to create non-legislative rules, they may not treat such rules as "binding" on the public.

(C) Members of the public should never rely on non-legislative rules.

(D) None of the above.

5.16. The Administrative Procedure Act does NOT require application of which of the following procedures to non-legislative rules?

(A) Notice and comment procedures.

(B) Publication in the *Federal Register* of "statements of general policy or interpretations of general applicability formulated and adopted by the agency."

(C) "A person may not in any manner be required to resort to, or be adversely affected by, a matter required to be published in the *Federal Register* and not so published" unless the person "has actual and timely notice of the terms of the matter."

(D) All of the above.

5.17. In *Chevron v. Natural Resources Defense Council, Inc.*, 467 U.S. 837 (1984), the Court held that:

(A) The power of an administrative agency to administer a congressionally created program necessarily requires the formulation of policy and the making of rules to fill any gap left, implicitly or explicitly, by Congress.

(B) If Congress has explicitly left a gap for an administrative agency to fill, there is an express delegation of authority to the agency to elucidate a specific provision of the statute by regulation.

(C) When Congress has made an implicit delegation of interpretive authority to an administrative agency, a court may not substitute its own construction of a statutory provision for a reasonable interpretation made by the administrator of an agency.

(D) All of the above.

5.18. Under *Chevron v. Natural Resources Defense Council, Inc.*, 467 U.S. 837 (1984), when Congress has explicitly left a gap in a regulatory scheme for the responsible administrative agency to fill by regulation, a reviewing court should give the interpretation the following weight:

(A) No weight, since, under the Court's landmark decision in *Marbury v. Madison*, 5 U.S. 137 (1803), it is emphatically the province and duty of the judiciary to say what the law is.

(B) Controlling weight unless it is arbitrary, capricious, or manifestly contrary to the statute.

(C) The weight it deserves based on the thoroughness evident in its consideration, the validity of its reasoning, its consistency with earlier and later pronouncements, and all those factors which give it power to persuade, if lacking power to control.

(D) None of the above.

5.19. In *Skidmore v. Swift & Co.*, 323 U.S. 134 (1944), the Court held that the rulings, interpretations, and opinions of the head of an administrative agency:

(A) While not controlling upon the courts by reason of their authority, do constitute a body of experience and informed judgment to which courts and litigants may properly resort for guidance.

(B) Are binding on the courts.

(C) Must be accepted by the courts if, but only if, they are reasonable and do not otherwise conflict with Congress' plainly stated intent.

(D) None of the above.

5.20. In determining the weight to give to an administrative interpretation under *Skidmore v. Swift & Co.*, 323 U.S. 134 (1944), which of the following statements best describes the judicial approach:

(A) Courts focus primarily on whether the interpretation is consistent with congressional intent.

(B) Courts focus primarily on the importance attached by the agency to the statement.

(C) Courts focus on the thoroughness evident in its consideration, the validity of its reasoning, its consistency with earlier and later pronouncements, and all those factors which give it power to persuade, if lacking power to control.

(D) None of the above.

5.21. In determining whether *Chevron v. Natural Resources Defense Council, Inc.*, 467 U.S. 837 (U.S. 1984), deference or *Skidmore v. Swift & Co.*, 323 U.S. 134 (1944), deference should apply in a given case, the United States Supreme Court places primary emphasis on the following factors:

(A) The agency's wishes.

(B) The format in which the agency's interpretation is revealed (e.g., legislative rule versus press release).

(C) The preferences of the reviewing judge.

(D) None of the above.

5.22. In *Christensen v. Harris County*, 529 U.S. 576 (2000), the Court declared that *Skidmore v. Swift & Co.*, 323 U.S. 134 (1944), deference should be accorded to:

(A) Interpretations set forth in legislative rules.

(B) Interpretations set forth in opinion letters issued by agencies.

(C) Interpretations set forth in adjudicative decisions.

(D) All of the above.

5.23. A non-legislative rule becomes a legislative rule when:

(A) The rule interprets a regulatory scheme.

(B) The rule purports to create a "binding duty" on regulated entities.

(C) Only when the agency says so.

(D) None of the above.

5.24. An agency issues a non-legislative rule (e.g., a policy statement) interpreting a regulatory scheme. Does it make sense for a regulated entity to conform its conduct with the requirements of the policy statement? Please write a short answer advising the regulated entity.

ANSWER:

5.25. A regulated entity relies on an agency's policy statement interpreting a regulatory scheme. When the agency alters its policy statement to the regulated entity's detriment, the company seeks to challenge the shift in positions. Please write a short answer stating whether a court is likely to allow the regulated entity to alter its interpretation under these circumstances.

ANSWER:

5.26. In *Bowles v. Seminole Sand & Rock Co.*, 325 U.S. 410 (1945), the Court held that:

(A) Agencies are entitled to exercise unfettered discretion over those they regulate.

(B) When an agency has interpreted a statute through an adjudicative decision, the agency's interpretation is of controlling weight unless it is plainly erroneous or inconsistent with the statute.

(C) When an agency has interpreted its own regulation, and a court is called on to interpret it, the ultimate criterion is the administrative interpretation which becomes of controlling weight unless it is plainly erroneous or inconsistent with the regulation.

(D) None of the above.

5.27. Based on recent decisions, it is safe to say that it would never be appropriate for a court to defer to an administrative interpretation stated in the form of:

(A) A citation issued by OSHA to a regulated entity issued as part of administrative proceedings before the Occupational Safety and Health Review Commission.

(B) A citation contained only in an adjudicative decision.

(C) An agency's interpretation of its own regulations that is contained in an amicus brief.

(D) All of the above.

6.1. In order to have jurisdiction to review administrative action, a court must:

(A) Have a statutory grant of jurisdiction.

(B) Have a plaintiff before it who has standing to bring the case.

(C) Have a case before it that is ripe for review.

(D) All of the above.

6.2. Which of the following statements are true regarding judicial jurisdiction to review administrative action?

(A) The general federal jurisdictional statute ("the district courts shall have original jurisdiction of all civil actions arising under the Constitution, laws, or treaties of the United States") can be used to establish jurisdiction.

(B) The APA's review provisions can be regarded as creating a general judicial grant of jurisdiction to review administrative action.

(C) The agency's governing statute is unlikely to contain a grant of jurisdiction to review the agency's action.

(D) None of the above.

6.3. In order to seek review of administrative action, a plaintiff must also establish a cause of action. Which of the following statements correctly indicates the law regarding causes of action to review administrative action?

(A) When an agency's governing statute contains a provision granting judicial review, the statute may also create a cause of action.

(B) Courts have inherent authority to review administrative action and can assert common law authority to establish causes of action.

(C) The APA cannot be used as the basis for establishing a cause of action.

(D) None of the above.

6.4. To successfully establish a cause of action under the APA, a plaintiff must be able to show which of the following:

(A) That the matter has not been excluded from review.

(B) That plaintiff has suffered a "legal wrong" or has been "adversely affected or aggrieved . . . within the meaning of a relevant statute."

(C) That the matter is specifically reviewable by statute or that it constitutes "final agency action for which there is no adequate remedy at law."

(D) All of the above.

6.5. In addition to establishing jurisdiction and a cause of action, a plaintiff must show which of the following elements in order to challenge administrative action:

(A) That he/she has exhausted his/her administrative remedies.

(B) That the case is "ripe" for review.

(C) That the matter is not "moot."

(D) All of the above.

6.6. The "standing" doctrine is based upon:

(A) The commerce clause.

(B) The "due process" clause.

(C) Article III's "case and controversy" requirement.

(D) All of the above.

6.7. In order to establish standing to sue, plaintiff must show which of the following:

(A) That plaintiff has suffered injury and that a favorable court decision can redress that injury.

(B) That he/she is suffering "legal injury" meaning that he/she can show that the common law or a statute provides him/her a right not to be injured.

(C) That he/she is suffering "ideological injury."

(D) All of the above.

6.8. In *Sierra Club v. Morton*, 405 U.S. 727 (1972), the Sierra Club sought to challenge administrative action that it viewed as having an adverse effect on the environment. It did so based on its status as an organization interested in the environment. In *Sierra Club*, the Court held that:

(A) Injury to environmental, aesthetic and recreational interests cannot qualify as injury in fact.

(B) In order to show injury in fact, plaintiff must be able to show that he/she has suffered an actual dollar loss.

(C) Injury to environmental, aesthetic and recreational interests can qualify as injury in fact.

(D) None of the above.

6.9. Under the holding in *Sierra Club v. Morton*, 405 U.S. 727 (1972), public interest and associational groups sometimes establish standing to bring suit on behalf of their members. Please write a short answer indicating what such groups must show in order to act on behalf of their members.

ANSWER:

In *Simon v. Eastern Kentucky Welfare Rights Organization*, 426 U.S. 26 (1976), a welfare rights organization challenged an Internal Revenue Service (IRS) regulation that reduced the amount of free medical care that hospitals had to provide in order to qualify as tax exempt charitable organizations. For years, the IRS had interpreted its governing statute to require hospitals, as a condition of being granted tax exempt status, to accept patients in need of car who were unable to pay for such services. The new regulation allowed hospitals to retain their tax exempt status even they turned individuals away for nonemergency services as long as they provided emergency services to those who could not pay.

6.10. Please write a short answer discussing what the welfare rights organization must be able to show in order to establish standing.

ANSWER:

6.11. There has been much debate about whether one person can assert the rights of another person. Please write a short answer indicating what must be shown to allow one person to assert the rights of another.

ANSWER:

6.12. In *Lujan v. Defenders of Wildlife*, 504 U.S. 555 (1992), the Court held that:

(A) Plaintiff can establish standing under the Endangered Species Act by showing that she once visited crocodiles in Egypt, intended to do so again, and believes that administrative action might irreparably affect her ability to do so.

(B) Citizens always have standing to challenge administrative action under the Endangered Species Act.

(C) Plaintiff cannot establish standing under the Endangered Species Act by showing that she once visited crocodiles in Egypt, intended to do so again, and believes that administrative action might irreparably affect her ability to do so.

(D) None of the above.

In *Federal Election Commission v. Akins*, 524 U.S. 11 (1998), the Federal Election Commission (FEC) concluded that the American Israel Public Affairs Committee (AIPAC) was not a "political committee" within the meaning of the Federal Election Campaign Act of 1971. As a result of the FEC's conclusion, AIPAC was not required to register with the FEC, appoint a treasurer, keep track of the names and addresses of contributors, or file complex FEC reports. A group of voters brought suit challenging the conclusion.

6.13. In *Akins*, the Court held that:

(A) A group of voters does not have standing to challenge the Federal Election Commission's determination (that the American Israel Public Affairs Committee was not a "political committee" within the meaning of the Federal Election Campaign Act).

(B) A group of voters has standing to challenge the Federal Election Commission's determination (that the American Israel Public Affairs Committee was not a "political committee" within the meaning of the Federal Election Campaign Act).

(C) The Article III "case and controversy" requirement is prudential rather than jurisdictional.

(D) None of the above.

6.14. Section 701(a) of the Administrative Procedure Act provides that judicial review is inapplicable when:

(A) Congress chooses to preclude review by statute.

(B) Agency action is committed to agency discretion by law.

(C) Both of the above.

(D) Neither of the above.

6.15. In *Abbott Laboratories v. Gardner*, 387 U.S. 136 (1967), the Court held that the APA's judicial review provisions should be:

(A) Strictly interpreted to prohibit judicial review except where congressional intent to permit review is obvious.

(B) Unconstitutional.

(C) Hospitably interpreted to prohibit review only when there is "clear and convincing evidence" that Congress intended to restrict review.

(D) None of the above.

Under the Agricultural Marketing Agreement Act of 1937, the Secretary of Agriculture may issue milk market orders that establish the minimum price that handlers (entities that process dairy products) must pay to producers (dairy farmers) for their milk products. Among the Secretary's 45 milk market orders is an order providing that handlers can pay producers a lower price for "reconstituted milk" (milk that is made from mixing milk powder with water). A consumers group wishes to challenge the law on the basis that, if reconstituted milk can be sold in jugs and cartons like ordinary milk but at a lower price, poor people are more likely to purchase reconstituted milk.

6.16. Please write a short answer discussing whether the consumers group has standing to bring the challenge.

ANSWER:

6.17. Section 704 of the Administrative Procedure Act provides that:

(A) Regardless of what an agency's governing statute may provide, judicial review is limited to "final agency action for which there is no other adequate remedy."

(B) Interim judicial review of agency action is readily available.

(C) Absent a specific statutory provision, judicial review is limited to "final agency action for which there is no other adequate remedy."

(D) None of the above.

The Department of Commerce, through its Census Bureau, made adjustments to the 1990 census' count of the number of people who live in Massachusetts. The Secretary of Commerce submitted the revised census to who reported it to Congress for use in reapportioning the House of Representatives.

6.18. Please write a short answer discussing whether the Court held that the Department's submission of census results to the President constitutes final agency action.

ANSWER:

A prisoner in a federal institution filed a *pro se* complaint against prison officials alleging a violation of the Eighth Amendment prohibition against cruel and unusual punishment. In particular, the prisoner alleged "deliberate indifference" to his needs and medical condition resulting from a back operation and a history of psychiatric problems. Under the "Administrative Remedy Procedure for Inmates" at federal correctional institutions, a prisoner may "seek formal review of a complaint which relates to any aspect of his imprisonment." The Procedure includes rapid filing and response timetables.

6.19. Please write a short answer discussing whether the prisoner should be required to exhaust his administrative remedies.

ANSWER:

Congress amended the Federal Food, Drug, and Cosmetic Act to require manufacturers of prescription drugs to print the "established name" of the drug "prominently and in type at least half as large as that used thereon for any proprietary name or designation for such drug," on labels and other printed material. The underlying purpose of the amendment was to make doctors and patients aware of the fact that many of the drugs sold under familiar trade names are actually identical to drugs sold under their "established" or less familiar trade names at significantly lower prices. Following the amendment, the FDA promulgated the following regulation for the "efficient enforcement" of the Act:

> If the label of a prescription drug bears a proprietary name or designation for the drug or any ingredient thereof, the established name, if such there be, corresponding to such proprietary name or designation, shall accompany each appearance of such proprietary name or designation. The regulation is enforceable through criminal sanctions.

A group of 37 individual drug manufacturers challenged the regulations on the ground that the FDA exceeded its authority by promulgating an order requiring labels, advertisements, and other printed matter relating to prescription drugs to designate the established name of the particular drug involved every time its trade name is used anywhere in such material. Claiming that they would suffer immediate injury from being forced to incur the cost of printing new prescription labels, the manufacturers sought preliminary and permanent injunctive relief prohibiting enforcement of the new regulation.

The government sought dismissal of the suit on ripeness grounds.

6.20. Please write a short answer discussing whether the case should be dismissed on ripeness grounds.

ANSWER:

The National Forest Management Act (NFMA) requires the Secretary of Agriculture to "develop, maintain, and . . . revise land and resource management plans for units of the National Forest System." When NFMA developed a federal land and resource management plan for the Wayne National Forest, the Sierra Club challenged the plan on the ground that the plan permitted too much logging and too much clearcutting. The Club sought declaratory and injunctive relief declaring the plan invalid and prohibiting NFMA from implementing it. NFMA moved to dismiss the suit on ripeness grounds because it had not focused upon a particular site, proposed a specific harvesting method, prepared an environmental review, and permitted the public an opportunity to be heard.

6.21. Please write a short answer describing whether the case is ripe for review.

ANSWER:

An FDA regulation provided that the Commissioner may "immediately suspend" FDA approval to market a product containing a color additive if the manufacturer refused to permit FDA inspectors "free access to all manufacturing facilities, processes, and formulae" involved in the process of producing the product. The Toilet Goods Association, which represents cosmetic manufacturers, seeks pre-enforcement review of the rule on the ground that the FDA lacked the authority to promulgate the rule. The FDA objects on ripeness grounds since it has not moved to enforce the regulation.

6.22. Please write a short answer discussing whether the case is ripe notwithstanding a movement to enforce?

ANSWER:

7.1. Administrative agencies are:

(A) Usually part of the judicial branch of government;

(B) Usually established as an arm of Congress;

(C) Usually part of the executive branch of government;

(D) An independent fourth branch of government.

Panama Refining Co. v. Ryan, 293 U.S. 388 (1935) involved the National Industrial Recovery Act (NIRA) which authorized the President to prohibit the transportation in interstate commerce of petroleum produced or withdrawn from storage in excess of the amount permitted by state law.

7.2. In *Panama Refining*, the United States Supreme Court held that:

(A) Administrative agencies should be given broad discretion to receive and implement powers delegated by Congress.

(B) In order to delegate power to administrative agencies, Congress must provide an "ineligible principle" in the form of a policy, standard or rule to guide the agency in the exercise of its discretion.

(C) The findings of administrative agency should be given controlling weight unless they are inconsistent with congressional intent.

(D) None of the above.

In *A.L.A. Schechter Poultry Corp. v. United States*, 295 U.S. 495 (1935), Congress authorized the President to approve codes of fair competition established by industry firms. However, the President could approve only if the code was written by representative group of businesses, did not promote monopolies, and if it served the objectives of the statute.

7.3. In *Schechter*, the Court held that:

(A) Congress has unquestioned authority to delegate power to the President to approve codes of fair competition.

(B) Congress may not delegate authority to the President to approve codes of fair competition without supplying an intelligible principle that limits the President's authority.

(C) Because of separation of power principles, Congress may never delegate legislative authority to the Executive branch.

(D) None of the above.

7.4. Under modern constitutional and administrative law principles, it is safe to say that both *Panama Refining Co. v. Ryan*, 293 U.S. 388 (1935), and *A.L.A. Schechter Poultry Corp. v. United States*, 295 U.S. 495 (1935), are decisions that can be described as:

(A) Having continuing currency and vitality.

(B) Having been lost in the dust bin of history.

(C) About to stage a comeback.

(D) None of the above.

7.5. In determining whether an "intelligible principle" exists, the Court has suggested that:

(A) Precise delineation of the principle, as dictated by decisions like *Panama Refining Co. v. Ryan*, 293 U.S. 388 (1935) and *A.L.A. Schechter Poultry Corp. v. United States*, 295 U.S. 495 (1935), is required.

(B) General delineation of the principle is all that is necessary.

(C) Courts are generally unable to find an "intelligible principle" in most delegations.

(D) None of the above.

7.6. Unlike legislative power, which cannot be delegated absent an "intelligible principle," judicial power can be regarded as:

(A) Vested by Article III of the United States Constitution solely in the judicial branch of government, and therefore are not delegable to other branches of government.

(B) Delegable to other branches of government, but only in conjunction with "intelligible principles."

(C) Are delegable provided that they involve "public rights" rather than "private rights."

(D) None of the above.

7.7. In *Crowell v. Benson*, 285 U.S. 22 (1932), the Court held that:

(A) The court distinguished between public rights and private rights.

    (B)   The case involved a private right because it involved the liability of one party to another.

    (C)   There had been a long history of juries, masters, and commissioners serving as fact finders subject to appellate review by Article III judges.

    (D)   All of the above.

7.8.   A "public right" involves the following:

    (A)   A right granted to the general public.

    (B)   A right granted to the government on behalf of the people.

    (C)   Rights which arise between the government and persons subject to its authority in connection with the performance of the constitutional functions of the executive or legislative departments.

    (D)   None of the above.

7.9.   In *Crowell v. Benson*, 285 U.S. 22 (1932), the Court also held that:

    (A)   Although the public rights/private rights distinction is important, courts should not slavishly adhere to it.

    (B)   Despite the public rights/private rights distinction, Congress should make every effort to assign judicial power solely to Article III courts.

    (C)   Congress could not delegated authority over "constitutional facts" to non-Article III bodies.

    (D)   None of the above.

7.10. In *Commodity Futures Trading Commission v. Schor*, 478 U.S. 833 (1986), the United States Supreme Court held that:

    (A)   The Commodity Futures Trading Commission (CFTC) could hear state law counterclaims in reparation proceedings.

    (B)   Held that the private rights/public rights distinction should always be treated as determinative in deciding whether adjudicative power could be delegated to a non-Article III body.

    (C)   A delegation to the CFTC posed a substantial threat to the concept of separation of powers.

    (D)   None of the above.

7.11. The Seventh Amendment to the United States Constitution provides that:

(A) Administrative agencies shall not impose cruel and unusual punishments.

(B) In suits at common law, where the value in controversy shall exceed $20, the right to jury trial shall be preserved.

(C) Administrative agencies shall not hold individuals on excessive bail.

(D) None of the above.

7.12. In *Atlas Roofing Co. v. Occupational Safety and Health Review Commission*, 430 U.S. 442 (1977), the Court held that:

(A) The Seventh Amendment mandates a jury trial before an administrative agency can impose a financial penalty under the Occupational Safety and Health Act.

(B) The Seventh Amendment does not mandate a jury trial before an administrative agency can impose a financial penalty under the Occupational Safety and Health Act.

(C) Even when Congress creates new statutory rights, it may not assign those rights to an administrative agency in which a jury trial would be incompatible.

(D) None of the above.

7.13. In *Atlas Roofing Co. v. Occupational Safety and Health Review Commission*, 430 U.S. 442 (1977), the Court also held that:

(A) When Congress creates new statutory "public rights," it may assign the adjudication of those rights to an administrative agency with which a jury trial would be incompatible.

(B) Congress can assign the adjudication of rights to an administrative body, to be heard without a jury, even though a jury would have been required had the case been heard by an Article III court.

(C) Administrative adjudication of public rights does not constitute a suit at common law and is not in the nature of such a suit.

(D) All of the above.

Suppose that Congress is concerned about the wisdom and content of administrative regulations. In an effort to gain more control over the administrative process, Congress passes a law authorizing either house of Congress to unilaterally "veto" new administrative rules.

7.14. Please write a short answer discussing the constitutionality of the new law.

ANSWER:

7.15. Please write a short answer describing the President's power to remove "officers" of the United States. Is Congress' "consent" required for removal, and may Congress stipulate that officers may only be removed for "cause?"

ANSWER:

7.16. Please write a short answer analyzing whether Federal Trade Commission commissioners are "officers" of the United States, and whether Congress can prevent the President from removing them except for "cause."

ANSWER:

For many years, federal legislation provided for the appointment of independent counsel to investigate allegations of misconduct by high ranking governmental officials. The independent counsel served in the United States Department of Justice.

7.17. Please write a short answer describing whether the independent counsel is an "officer" of the United States and whether Congress can prohibit removal of an independent counsel except for cause.

ANSWER:

Congress wants to establish the Federal Election Commission to enforce federal campaign finance laws. However, Congress does not wish to allow the President to appoint all of the members for fear that the FEC will persecute the President's opponents.

7.18. Please write a short answer discussing whether the Congress can reserve to itself the power to nominate some commission members.

ANSWER:

8.1. Agencies conduct inspections, require the submission of reports, and issue subpoenas, for which of the following reasons:

   (A) To gain information needed by them and Congress to set policy.

   (B) To gain information needed to enforce regulatory requirements.

   (C) To gain information needed to prosecute companies for civil and criminal violations.

   (D) All of the above.

8.2. Inspections are performed by a variety of administrative agencies for a variety of reasons including the following:

   (A) Health inspectors enter restaurants to ensure that food storage, preparation, and service areas are clean.

   (B) Child welfare officials enter homes searching for abused or neglected children.

   (C) Occupational Safety and Health Administration inspectors examine construction and work sites to make sure that workers are employed in safe and healthy conditions.

   (D) All of the above.

8.3. Under the Fourth Amendment, which of the following principles govern administrative inspections?

   (A) Because administrative searches are conducted for health and safety reasons, rather than to search for evidence of criminal activity, the Fourth Amendment's prohibition against "unreasonable searches and seizures" does not apply.

   (B) Because of a long tradition of regulatory and administrative inspections, a warrant is not required.

   (C) Even though administrative inspections are conducted for health and safety reasons, the Fourth Amendment prohibition against "unreasonable searches and seizures" is fully applicable.

(D)   None of the above.

8.4.   In its landmark decision in *Camara v. Municipal Court*, 387 U.S. 523 (1967), the United States Supreme Court held that:

(A)   Administrative searches are subject to the Fourth Amendment prohibition against "unreasonable searches and seizures."

(B)   Administrative searches are subject to the Fourth Amendment's requirement of a warrant based upon probable cause.

(C)   Administrative searches can involve significant intrusions on personal privacy.

(D)   All of the above.

8.5.   In *Camara v. Municipal Court*, 387 U.S. 523 (1967), in imposing the requirement of a warrant based on probable cause, the Court emphasized that:

(A)   Administrative searches and inspections should be treated like any other search so that the warrant and probable cause requirements should be strictly enforced.

(B)   Because administrative searches target ordinary citizens and businesses, rather than criminals (who are targeted in ordinary criminal searches), the requirement of a warrant based on probable cause was especially necessary and should not be compromised.

(C)   Because administrative searches and inspections do not involve searches for evidence of criminal activity, the probable cause requirement can be modified to require only a reasonable inspection plan and proof that it is time to inspect under that plan (as opposed to the ordinary requirement of proof that the fruits, instrumentalities of evidence of crime exist and can be found at the place to be searched).

(D)   None of the above.

8.6.   Because of *Camara v. Municipal Court*'s (387 U.S. 523 (1967)) requirement of a warrant, the following can be said of modern administrative inspections:

(A)   Most administrative inspections are conducted pursuant to a warrant.

(B)   Most administrative inspectors begin their day before a magistrate seeking warrants.

(C)   Although the Fourth Amendment requires a warrant and probable cause in order to conduct an administrative inspection, few inspections are actually based on a warrant because the individual or business being inspected usually gives consent to the search.

(D)   None of the above.

8.7. The following businesses can be regarded as closely regulated industries and therefore subjected to warrantless searches:

(A) Liquor dealers.

(B) Firearms dealers.

(C) Underground mines.

(D) All of the above.

When the police conduct an illegal inspection in violation of the Fourth Amendment, a variety of remedies might be available including civil actions and criminal prosecutions. Another potential remedy is the exclusionary evidence rule which precludes the use of illegally obtained evidence.

8.8. Please write a short answer describing whether the exclusionary evidence rule automatically applies in administrative proceedings.

ANSWER:

8.9. Is it safe to say that the exclusionary evidence rule should never be applied in administrative proceedings? Please write a short answer discussing the situations in which the rule might apply.

ANSWER:

8.10. In *United States v. Janis*, 428 U.S. 433 (1976), the Court found that the costs of exclusion outweighed the benefits because:

(A) There is very little benefit ever to be obtained from applying the exclusionary evidence rule in civil proceedings.

(B) Civil proceedings are less important than criminal proceedings.

(C) The evidence in *Janis* was seized by the police for use in criminal proceedings, but used by the IRS in civil proceedings, and the Court concluded that the police incentive to seize related to the criminal proceeding (and that little additional incentive existed to seize the evidence merely for use a civil enforcement proceeding).

(D) None of the above.

Following *United States v. Janis*, 428 U.S. 433 (1976), many commentators believed that the exclusionary evidence rule might apply in civil proceedings when the case involved an intra-agency application. In other words, if the *Janis* evidence had been seized by the IRS itself for use in the civil proceeding, then one could hope to deter the IRS by applying the exclusionary rule in the civil proceeding. Although the commentators are undoubtedly correct, the Court refused to apply the exclusionary rule to an intra-agency violation in *INS v. Lopez-Mendoza*, 468 U.S 1032 (1984).

8.11. The Court justified its refusal to apply the exclusionary rule on the following grounds:

(A) The benefits of exclusion are low because, even if the INS acted illegally, the government can still impose the remedy of deportation.

(B) The benefits of exclusion are low because the overwhelming majority of deportation proceedings end in voluntary deportation.

(C) The benefits of exclusion are low because the INS has its own comprehensive system for deterring violations.

(D) All of the above.

8.12. In addition to conducting inspections, agencies also impose record keeping and reporting requirements on regulated entities. Which of the following statements accurately summarizes the authority of administrative agencies to impose such requirements?

(A) Administrative agencies possess inherent authority to impose record keeping and reporting requirements.

(B) Administrative agencies can only impose record keeping and reporting requirements when based on explicit statutory authorization.

(C) Administrative agencies can only impose record keeping and reporting requirements based on explicit or implicit statutory authorization.

(D) None of the above.

8.13. Which of the following statements accurately describes the Paperwork Reduction Act?

(A) The Act regulates the "collection of information" by agencies including "the obtaining, causing to be obtained, soliciting, or requiring the disclosure to third parties or the public, of facts or opinions by or for an agency, regardless of form or format, calling for answers from ten or more persons.

(B) The Act requires agencies to review each proposed collection information requirement to ensure that it contains an evaluation of the need for collection of the information.

(C) The Act requires a specific objectively supported estimate of the burden the collection will impose on persons (measured in hours).

(D) All of the above.

8.14. Agencies also have the power to issue subpoenas for information. Which of the following statements accurately describes the power of administrative agencies to issue subpoenas?

(A) Agencies can only subpoena documents when they have probable cause to believe that the documents contain "evidence" of legal violations.

(B) Agencies can subpoena documents when the disclosure would be "reasonable."

(C) Agencies can never subpoena documents when the request involves nothing more than a "fishing expedition" for evidence of legal violations.

(D) None of the above.

A government agency seeks to compel a hospital to produce documents and other information. The hospital's patients are concerned because they fear that their confidential information might be revealed.

8.15. Please write a short answer discussing whether the patients (as third parties) can object to the disclosure on privacy grounds.

ANSWER:

8.16. Please write a short answer describing the Fifth Amendment Privilege against Self-Incrimination's application to subpoenas.

ANSWER:

8.17. Which of the following statements correctly states how the Fifth Amendment Privilege against Self-Incrimination applies?

(A) The Privilege can be used to resist the production of documents when the mere act of production, as opposed to the contents of the documents, would incriminate the person producing the documents.

(B) Under *Securities and Exchange Commission v. Dresser Industries, Inc.*, 628 F.2d 1368 (D.C. Cir. 1980), the Privilege provides regulated entities with the basis for objecting to being required to simultaneously defend both civil and criminal proceedings.

(C) The Privilege has no application in administrative proceedings.

(D) All of the above.

9.1. The Freedom of Information Act (FOIA) provides that:

   (A) Administrative agencies must provide information free of charge to citizens who request it.

   (B) Agencies, upon any request for records which reasonably describes such records and is made in accordance with published rules stating the time, place, fees (if any), and procedures to be followed, shall make the records promptly available to any person."

   (C) Both of the above.

   (D) Neither of the above.

9.2. The FOIA requires an agency that receives a request for information to:

   (A) Decide within twenty days whether to comply with the request.

   (B) If it denies the request, provide the person with an explanation and inform the person of any internal appeal opportunities.

   (C) If the person appeals, decide the case within 20 days.

   (D) All of the above.

9.3. Which of the following exceptions apply under the FOIA?

   (A) Classified information.

   (B) Internal agency personnel rules and practices.

   (C) Information specifically exempted from disclosure by statute.

   (D) All of the above.

9.4. Under the FOIA, agencies can impose which of the following fees for document search and production?

   (A) "Fair and equitable" charges for searches and production.

    (B) Fees to recover the direct cost of searching, duplicating, and reviewing commercial requests.

    (C) Reasonable charges for costs associated with "resolving issues of law or policy" related to FOIA requests.

    (D) None of the above.

9.5. If an agency denies a FOIA request, the requester is then:

    (A) Prohibited from seeking judicial review by the terms of FOIA.

    (B) May seek judicial review.

    (C) May seek judicial review, but only after asking the agency to reconsider.

    (D) None of the above.

9.6. Under the FOIA, when review is sought of a denial, which of the following rules apply?

    (A) The defendant agency bears the burden of proving that the documents are exempt from disclosure.

    (B) A reviewing court must determine the case *de novo*.

    (C) If the plaintiff substantially prevails, he/she is entitled to an award of attorney's fees and costs.

    (D) All of the above.

9.7. The FOIA is available to:

    (A) Citizens and residents of the United States.

    (B) Foreign citizens, corporations and governments.

    (C) Non-resident aliens.

    (D) All of the above.

9.8. In order to invoke the FOIA, the requester:

    (A) Must be able to show a definite need for the requested information and documents.

    (B) Must be able to show a "likelihood" that the requested information and documents will produce information that he/she needs.

    (C) Need not make any showing of need.

(D) None of the above.

9.9. In order to invoke the FOIA, the request:

(A) Can be stated in general terms.

(B) Must "reasonably describe" the information and documents sought.

(C) Both of the above.

(D) None of the above.

10.1. Regarding attorney's fees in cases against federal agencies, which of the following is generally true?

    (A)   In the absence of some other statutory authorization, prevailing parties generally must bear the costs of their legal representation.

    (B)   Contingency fee arrangements are prohibited.

    (C)   Citizen suit provisions rarely include statutory authorization to award costs, including attorney fees to prevailing parties.

    (D)   None of the above.

10.2. Regarding the types of proceedings in which the Equal Access to Justice Act authorizes, if appropriate, the recovery of fees and other expenses including attorney's fees, which of the following is the least accurate statement?

    (A)   The Act empowers federal courts to grant awards in actions filed in federal court seeking judicial review of agency action pursuant to the APA.

    (B)   The Act empowers federal courts to exercise their discretion and grant awards in actions filed in federal court by agencies alleging violations of their regulatory programs.

    (C)   The Act does not authorize awards in agency proceedings involving the granting or renewing of a license.

    (D)   The Act authorizes awards in all agency adjudications at which the government is represented by counsel.

Assume that, following an initial denial of social security disability benefits, the claimant requested an ALJ hearing. At the hearing, the claimant provided the oral testimony of her physician and oncologist. The ALJ affirmed the denial. The claimant properly sought judicial review of the agency determination in federal district court.

10.3. Assuming that the district court has set aside and reversed the denial of benefits (and assuming no statutory authorization for costs or fees other than the Equal Access to Justice Act), which of the following is an accurate statement ?

(A) Upon proper application, the court shall award to the claimant fees and other expenses and costs incurred by the party in the litigation — unless the court finds that the agency position was substantially justified.

(B) The court may award to the claimant fees and expenses of attorneys — unless the court finds that the agency position was substantially justified.

(C) The court may award to the claimant the costs incurred by the party in the litigation — unless the court finds that the agency position was substantially justified.

(D) The court shall include in the award to the claimant the fees and other expenses incurred by the claimant in the ALJ hearing if the court finds that the agency position was not substantially justified.

10.4. When an award for fees and expenses under the Equal Access to Justice Act hinges on whether the position of the United States was substantially justified, which of the following is an accurate statement?

(A) A court may find that the agency position in a civil action was "substantially justified" if the position had "some substance and a fair possibility of success."

(B) A court may find that the agency position in a civil action was "substantially justified" as long as the position had sufficient support to preclude a finding of frivolousness.

(C) A court may find that the agency position in a civil action was "substantially justified" if the position was justified to a degree that could satisfy a reasonable person, and had a reasonable basis both in law and in fact.

(D) Both (A) and (B) are accurate.

Assume that the Occupational Safety and Health Administration (OSHA) has brought an enforcement proceeding against an employer who has allegedly violated certain safety standards promulgated by OSHA, given OSHA's interpretation of those standards; and that OSHA proceedings must follow the APA's formal adjudication procedures. Assume also that the employer lost at the ALJ hearing, but prevailed at the appeal to the Occupational Safety and Health Review Commission (OSHRC). The employer, as the prevailing party, has submitted an application for an award of fees and other expenses.

10.5. Regarding recovery of fees and other expenses under the Equal Access to Justice Act, which of the following is an accurate statement?

(A) If the employer's application for an award of fees and other expenses was filed within thirty days of the OSHRC decision, the agency must award to the employer, as the prevailing party, fees and other expenses incurred in connection with the agency proceedings.

(B)   If the employer's application for an award of fees and other expenses was filed within thirty days of the OSHRC decision, the agency must determine whether the award is proper.

(C)   If the employer's application for an award of fees and other expenses was filed within thirty days of the OSHRC decision, the decision whether the award is proper will be deferred if OSHA appeals the merits of the adjudication.

(D)   If the employer's application for an award of fees and other expenses was filed within thirty days of the OSHRC decision, the employer has a right to submit additional evidence showing that OSHA's position was not substantially justified.

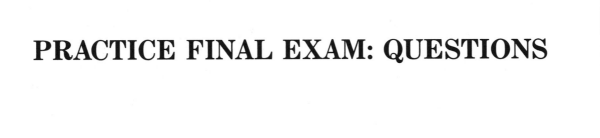

PRACTICE FINAL EXAM: QUESTIONS

INSTRUCTIONS: Suggested time for the examination is 2 hours.

1.1. An independent counsel is regarded as an inferior official, rather than as an officer of the United States, because:

    (A) His duties are essentially executive in nature and are of a type normally performed by executive branch officials.

    (B) He has limited jurisdiction and tenure.

    (C) He lacks policymaking or significant administrative authority.

    (D) All of the above.

1.2. Beginning with President Reagan, presidents of the United States have, through Executive Orders, tried to centralize oversight of agency rulemaking and to enhance planning and coordination of rulemaking. Regarding Executive Order 12,866 and the role of the Office of Management and Budget (OMB) and the Office of Information and Regulatory Affairs (OIRA), which of the following is NOT an accurate statement?

    (A) OMB and OIRA have authority to review an agency's rulemaking plans to ensure consistency with the President's priorities.

    (B) OBM and OIRA have authority to require agencies to assess the potential costs and benefits of significant regulatory actions.

    (C) OMB and OIRA have the final authority to disapprove of any regulatory scheme selected by an agency which fails to maximize net benefits.

    (D) OMB and OIRA may require agencies to re-assess the need for, and appropriateness of, existing, significant regulations.

1.3. Regarding agency action generally, which of the following is a correct statement?

    (A) When an agency engages in rule making, the APA rarely dictates that formal trial-like procedures are required.

    (B) When an agency engages in adjudication, the APA almost always dictates that formal trial-like procedures are required.

(C)   If the APA's formal trial-like procedures are not applicable to agency adjudication, the agency is free to use whatever procedures it deems appropriate.

(D)   When an agency engages in rule making, the agency need only follow either the APA's formal trial-like procedures or the APA's informal notice and comment procedures.

1.4.   Explain aspects of Executive Order 12,866 which tend to curb or provide a safeguard against undue influence by OMB or the President.

ANSWER:

Assume that, following an initial denial of social security disability benefits, the claimant requested an ALJ hearing. At the hearing, the claimant provided the oral testimony of her physician and oncologist. The ALJ affirmed the denial. The claimant properly sought judicial review of the agency determination in federal district court.

1.5.   Assuming that the district court upholds the denial of benefits (and assuming no statutory authorization for costs or fees other than the Equal Access to Justice Act), which of the following is an accurate statement?

(A)   Upon proper application, the court shall award to the agency the fees and other expenses and costs incurred by the agency in the litigation — unless the court finds that the claimant's position was substantially justified.

(B)   The court may award to the agency fees and expenses of attorneys — unless the court finds that the claimant's position was substantially justified.

(C)   The court may award to the agency the costs incurred by the agency in the litigation.

(D)   None of the above.

1.6.   Assume that the automobile industry wants the Department of Transportation to modify a rule pertaining to use of airbags in compact vehicles, and files a formal, written petition requesting amendment. Regarding the industry's petition, which of the following is an accurate statement?

(A)   The agency is free to ignore the request.

(B)   The agency may postpone acting on the request, even for several years, without triggering a right to judicial review.

(C)   A denial of the request will not be set aside even if the agency has conducted little investigation into the advisability of the amendment, if the agency, in a written explanation, points to other priorities requiring agency attention.

(D)   The agency may deny the request without expressly explaining why.

Assume that the National Park Service ("NPS") has waived its § 553(a) exemption; and, further, assume that, following proper notice and comment procedures, NPS promulgated a rule which banned the use of snowmobiles in national parks. The proceeding, however, took more time than the NPS anticipated. The Final Rule, along with its general statement of basis and purpose, was published in the Federal Register on February 3, 2004. On March 1st, a snowmobiling group called Freedom Riders, in protest of the ban, led a highly publicized parade of snowmobiles through Yellowstone National Park. NPS rangers issued citations to the fifty riders who participated in the parade, imposing a $300 fine for violation of the new ban.

1.7. Regarding the NPS enforcement of the new ban, which of the following is an accurate statement?

(A) The citations are valid because the NPS published the Final Rule banning snowmobiles in national parks in the Federal Register.

(B) The citations are not valid because, under the APA, the new rule banning snowmobiles in national parks could not have been effective on March 1st.

(C) The citations are valid because the Freedom Riders had actual notice of the terms of the new rule banning snowmobiles in national parks.

(D) None of the above.

1.8. Explain a key difference between executive agencies and independent agencies.
ANSWER:

1.9. Which of the following is NOT an agency adjudication?

(A) A Chicago police officer, responding to a complaint, determined that a car parked on a city street was "junk" and, pursuant to city policy, left a sticker on the car explaining that, if the car was not moved within 72 hours it would be disposed of as scrap.

(B) A decision by the Federal Housing Authority (FHA) to terminate Capital Mortgage Inc.'s authority to originate single family home mortgages insured by FHA.

(C) A city's decision (pursuant to and in conformity with a statute authorizing municipalities to assess a variety of taxes) that property owners in a certain township, who would benefit from construction of a road, should pay a special tax or fee.

(D) A determination by the National Transportation Safety Board (NTSB) that a flight instructor's pilot certificate should be suspended for violation of statutory aircraft maintenance standards.

1.10. Please write a short answer describing when, under *Camara v. Municipal Court*, 387 U.S. 523 (1967), it is permissible to conduct warrantless administrative inspections.

ANSWER:

1.11. The "standing" doctrine is premised on which of the following considerations?

(A) Article III's "case and controversy" requirement.

(B) Prudential concerns designed to ensure that courts do not exercise judicial power unnecessarily.

(C) Both of the above.

(D) None of the above.

1.12. "Retroactivity" is a doctrine that applies to:

(A) The retroactive application of criminal laws.

(B) The "retroactive" application of any law or judicial decision, or any agency rule, decision or policy.

(C) The retroactive application of legislation.

(D) Certain types of nuclear waste.

1.13. Under modern administrative law precedent, which of the following principles correctly states Congress' authority to delegate power to administrative agencies?

(A) The integrity and maintenance of the system of government ordained by the Constitution precludes Congress from delegating legislative power to another branch of government.

(B) Separation of powers principles, and checks and balances principles, prohibit Congress from delegating power to other branches of government.

(C) In determining what Congress may do in seeking assistance from another branch, the extent and character of that assistance must be fixed according to common sense and the inherent necessities of government coordination.

(D) None of the above.

In *Air Courier Conference of America v. American Postal Workers Union, AFL-CIO*, 498 U.S. 517 (1991), the United States Postal Service (USPS) decided to suspend the Private Express Statute (PES) to allow for international re-mailing. USPS employees, who believed that the decision would cost them jobs, sought to challenge the decision.

1.14. In *Air Courier*, the Court held that:

(A) Postal employees are not within the "zone of interest" of the Private Express Statute (PES) so that they may challenge the United States Postal Service's decision to suspend the PES for international re-mailing.

(B) Postal employees are within the "zone of interest" of the Private Express Statute (PES) so that they may challenge the United States Postal Service's decision to suspend the PES for international remailing.

(C) Federal employees never have standing to challenge the actions of the federal government.

(D) None of the above.

1.15. In order to be upheld, a delegation of power from Congress to a coordinate branch of government must be:

(A) Made with the assent of all three branches of government.

(B) Provide specific guidance so that the coordinate branch of government is called upon to do no more than implement, rather than formulate, policy.

(C) Accompanied by an intelligible principle to which the person or body authorized to [exercise the authority] is directed to conform.

(D) None of the above.

A trade association requested an opinion from the Department of Labor's Wage and Hour Division regarding whether coin-operated laundries were subject to the minimum wage and overtime laws. The Department responded with a letter indicating that the new law did indeed subject the laundries to the law.

1.16. Please write a short answer discussing whether the letter is ripe for review.

ANSWER:

1.17. In *Bowsher v. Synar*, 478 U.S. 714 (1986), the Court held that:

(A) Congress may supervise officers of the United States in their execution of the laws of the United States.

(B) Congress may reserve to itself the power to remove officers of the United States.

(C) Congress may not reserve to itself the power to remove officers of the United States.

(D) None of the above.

In *Chrysler Corp. v. Brown*, 441 U.S. 281 (1979), Chrysler Corp. sought to prevent the Defense Logistics Agency from releasing records to the Department of Labor. Chrysler claimed that it would suffer injury, because, following the release, federal rules would require disclosure under the FOIA.

1.18. Please write a short answer discussing whether the objection is valid.

ANSWER:

1.19. Which of the following statements correctly summarizes the procedures required for imposition of record keeping and reporting requirements?

   (A) Agencies can only impose record keeping and reporting requirements legislatively using notice and comment procedures.

   (B) Agencies can only impose record keeping and reporting requirements using adjudicative procedures.

   (C) Agencies can impose record keeping and reporting requirements in a variety of ways including rulemakings and orders.

   (D) None of the above.

1.20. Under the Equal Access to Justice Act, which of the following prevailing parties in an agency proceeding would be ineligible to recover fees and other expenses?

   (A) An individual with a net worth of $1 million.

   (B) A business with 800 employees and a net worth of $7 million.

   (C) A tax-exempt charitable organizations with a net worth of $10 million.

   (D) A city government with 400 employees and a net worth of $3 million.

Under the Medicare Act, hospitals are reimbursed for certain services provided to Medicare recipients. The Act authorizes Hospitals to appeal reimbursement decisions to the Provider Reimbursement Review Board (the Board) of the Department of Health and Human Services (HHS), and authorizes the Board to establish procedures to implement the provider right to appeals. The Board issued a rule which provides as follows: "A provider appealing a reimbursement determination must comply with the Board's schedule for submission of one or more position papers. If the provider fails to submit a final position paper to the Board by the scheduled due date, the Board may dismiss the appeal."

Assume that Memorial Hospital filed a timely appeal following a disallowance of approximately $290,000 of the reimbursement requested by Memorial Hospital. The Board's schedule of submissions required preliminary position papers by November 1, 2003 and final papers by February 1, 2004. Due to confusion within the hospital's administrative offices, Memorial Hospital failed to file either a preliminary or a final position paper. The Board thus dismissed

Memorial's appeal. Memorial Hospital has challenged the Board's rule regarding dismissal of appeals as being invalid because the Board failed to use notice and comment rulemaking procedures.

1.21. Which of the following is the most sound judicial response?

(A) The rule will not be set aside because it would have been impractical for the Board to use notice and comment procedures for a rule that merely prescribes the manner in which the parties present themselves to the agency.

(B) The rule will not be set aside because it does not alter the substantive standards the Board uses to review provider claims for reimbursement.

(C) The rule will be set aside because it has a sufficiently grave affect on the Hospital's substantive right to a hearing afforded by the Medicare Act.

(D) The rule will be set aside because choices concerning what "process is due" in adjudicatory agency actions necessarily encode substantive value judgments.

1.22. The Freedom of Information Act charges, except for duplicating charges, can be waived for which of the following:

(A) Citizens of the United States, but not non-citizens.

(B) Commercial entities which can show special need.

(C) Requests by the news media, or by educational or non-commercial scientific organization for scholarly or scientific research.

(D) None of the above.

1.23. Benjamin Gerson created a revocable trust to benefit his wife, Eleanor Gerson, and made his last changes to the instrument in 1983. By its terms the trust became irrevocable when Benjamin died three days later. The trust gave Eleanor the right to use the income during her life and to appoint a beneficiary to receive the corpus when she died. If Eleanor failed to use her appointment power, the corpus would flow into another trust for the benefit of Benjamin's children.

Eleanor died in 2000 with a will exercising the power of appointment and leaving the trust corpus to her grandchildren. After Eleanor's executor filed a tax return for the Estate, the Commissioner of the Internal Revenue Service (IRS) responded with a notice of deficiency, claiming that the transfer triggered the generation-skipping transfer (GST) tax. According to the IRS, the Gerson Estate owed $100,000. The Gerson Estate brought an action in the United States Tax Court to challenge the deficiency. The Tax Court agreed with the IRS.

On judicial review, the Estate argues that a provision in the Tax Reform Act of 1986 grandfathers certain trusts created before 1985. This statutory provision states that the tax does not apply to "any generation-skipping transfer under a trust which was irrevocable on September 25, 1985, but only to the extent that such transfer is not made out of corpus added to the trust after September 25, 1985." Because Eleanor never added any assets to the corpus, the Estate asserts that the provision disposes of the case.

The IRS Commissioner disagrees, however, reasoning that testators must have cast the die before 1985 by including the skip transfer in the trust instrument itself or conferring no more than a limited power of appointment. The IRS has embodied this view in a regulation, Treasury Regulation § 26.2601-1(b)(1)(i), which provides that the grandfather exception "does not apply to a transfer of property pursuant to the exercise, release, or lapse of a general power of appointment. . . ." Congress has delegated to Treasury authority to issue regulations, and this regulation was promulgated after notice and comment procedure.

The Estate argues that the interpretation is contrary to the plain language of the effective date provision. The IRS responds by arguing that its view is entitled to judicial deference. Regarding the agency's invocation of deference, which of the following is an accurate statement?

(A)   If the court disagrees with the Estate's "plain language" argument, the court must defer to the agency under *Chevron* because regulation § 26.2601-1(b)(1)(i) constitutes an agency interpretation of the statute the agency is charged with implementing.

(B)   If the court disagrees with the Estate's "plain language" argument, the court must apply *Chevron* deference to the agency's view because Congress delegated authority to the agency generally to make rules carrying the force of law, and regulation § 26.2601-1(b)(1)(i) was promulgated in the exercise of that authority.

(C)   Even if the court agrees with the Estate's "plain language" argument, the court must defer to the agency under *Chevron* and *Mead* because regulation § 26.2601-1(b)(1)(i) was promulgated pursuant to notice and comment.

(D)   Even if the court agrees with the Estate's "plain language" argument, *Chevron* deference is not triggered in this case because regulation § 26.2601-1(b)(1)(i) does not have the force of law.

The following fact pattern applies to Questions 1.24 and 1.25.

John and Jane Johnson have been living every parent's nightmare. Accused of abuse by a rebellious child, they were arrested and had their other children taken away from them. When a doctor confirmed that the abuse charges could not be true, the state dismissed the criminal case against them. Upon the Johnsons' petition, the court found them factually innocent of the charges for which they had been arrested, and ordered the arrest records sealed and destroyed. However, the Johnsons still had a problem. They had been previously placed on the state's Child Abuse Central Index ("the CACI"), a database of known or suspected child abusers.

The maintenance of the CACI is governed by the Child Abuse and Neglect Reporting Act ("CANRA"). CANRA mandates that various statutorily enumerated individuals report instances of known or suspected child abuse and neglect either to a law enforcement agency or to a child welfare agency. These agencies, in turn, are required to conduct "an active investigation," which involves investigating the allegations and determining whether the incident is "unfounded or not unfounded." CANRA also provides that these agencies must send to the state Department of Justice ("DOJ") a written report "of every case it investigates of known or suspected child abuse or severe neglect which is determined to be "not unfounded" (Child Abuse Reports). CANRA requires that the DOJ maintain an index of all Child Abuse Reports: this index, the CACI, is maintained by means of a computerized data bank.

CANRA states that the DOJ shall make the information in the CACI available to a broad range of third parties for a variety of purposes. For example, the information is provided to persons required by statute to make inquiries for purposes of pre-employment background investigations for teachers, child care licensing or employment, adoption, or child placement. CANRA provides that persons obtaining the CACI information are responsible for obtaining the a copy of the Child Abuse Report from the reporting agency, and for drawing independent conclusions regarding the quality of the evidence disclosed and whether sufficient evidence supports a conclusion that abuse is "not unfounded."

CANRA requires that, when an investigating agency forwards a Child Abuse Report to the DOJ, the agency shall also notify in writing the known or suspected child abuser that he or she has been reported to the CACI and provide information about how he or she may obtain a copy of the Child Abuse Report.

There is no provision for removing an individual listed in the CACI. Further, CANRA offers no procedure for challenging a listing on the CACI. CANRA does provide that "if a Child Abuse Report has previously been filed which subsequently proves to be unfounded," the DOJ shall be notified in writing of that fact and shall not retain the report. The statute does not describe who must notify the DOJ of that fact, or how the determination that a report has "subsequently prove[d] to be unfounded" is to be made. CANRA also provides that the CACI "shall be continually updated by the department and shall not contain any reports that are determined to be unfounded." By using the passive voice, CANRA fails to specify who is supposed to determine that a report is unfounded, or how to make that decision in order to remove unfounded reports from the CACI. CANRA also provides that "submitting agencies are responsible for the accuracy, completeness, and retention of Child Abuse Reports," thus suggesting that the investigating agencies are also somehow responsible for removing reports that are determined to be unfounded.

Although CANRA provides no procedure for an individual to challenge a CACI listing, presumably a listed person could request the original investigating agency to reconsider whether the initial finding was correct. Additionally, such a person could presumably request any inquiring agencies to conduct an independent investigation.

The Johnsons have filed an action in federal court, arguing that this regulatory scheme violates their Fourteenth Amendment right to procedural due process by listing and continuing to list them on the CACI, without any available process to challenge that listing. The Johnsons allege that listing them on CACI has harmed their reputation and burdened their ability to pursue some of their normal goals and activities. For example, they assert that they would like to work or volunteer at a neighborhood community center offering child care and a variety of other services and have proffered an affidavit from the Human Resources Manager at the center stating that all adults must undergo a CACI check prior to obtaining clearance to volunteer or teach at the center.

1.24. Regarding step-one of the relevant due process analysis, which of the following is an accurate statement?

(A) Procedural due process is not triggered on the facts presented because being placed on the CACI does not mean that the person has been found guilty of child abuse or neglect.

(B) Procedural due process is not triggered because, although the agency action arguably has harmed the Johnsons' reputations, it has not foreclosed future employment opportunities because information is accessible only to designated types of third parties and, further, inquiring third parties are cautioned to obtain Child Abuse Reports and to draw independent conclusions.

(C) Procedural due process is readily triggered on the facts because agency action has harmed the Johnsons' reputation and has foreclosed future employment opportunities by virtue of the Child Abuse Reports being available to and accessible by third parties required to conduct background checks.

(D) Procedural due process is not triggered because the Johnsons can bring a suit for defamation.

1.25. Without affecting your answer to the prior question, assume that the court determined that the CANRA regulatory scheme implicates the Johnsons' constitutionally protected liberty interest. Regarding step-two of the relevant due process analysis, which of the following is the most appropriate judicial response?

(A) The court should find a due process violation because unsubstantiated accusations impose a gravely serious burden on persons listed on the CACI and, further, the state does not have an interest in false information being included in the CACI.

(B) The court should not find a violation of due process because the state has a vital interest in preventing child abuse and an index such as CACI that includes reports when the allegations are "not unfounded" is crucial to protection of the state's interest.

(C) The court should not find a violation of due process because the state has a vital interest in preventing child abuse and an index such as CACI that includes reports when the allegations are "not unfounded" is crucial to protection of the state's interest, and, further, under the current scheme persons listed can ask the original investigating agency to reconsider its finding or ask "inquiring agencies" to conduct an independent investigation.

(D) The court should find a violation of due process because a finding that allegations are "not unfounded" is a very low threshold, thereby creating a unreasonably high risk of error, and, further, additional protections such as some type of hearing by which a person can compel a reconsideration upon some appropriate showing would not be too burdensome for the state.

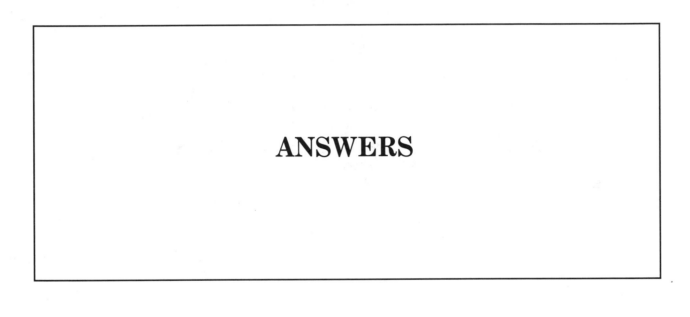

ANSWERS

1.1.   **Answer (C) is correct.** During the early years of the New Deal, the federal courts often were hostile to new regulatory programs. However, following President Roosevelt's thwarted "court-packing" plan, the Supreme Court and the lower courts swung from hostility to deference; resulting in a substantial curtailment of rigorous judicial review of agency action. As noted, the APA was intended to provide tools to more readily oversee and monitor agency action.

   Answer (A) is not correct. American administrative law grew out of the common law. As early as the seventeenth century, writs were used to control a growing number of administrative functions. However, laissez-faire principles prevailed from 1775–1875, when the role of administrative government was far less extensive than it is today. Beginning in 1875, the role of the administrative state grew, largely in the form of rate regulation of railroads and grain elevators. The Interstate Commerce Commission was established in 1887; and the Federal Trade Commission was created in 1914.

   Answer (B) is not correct. It is generally understood that the APA was enacted in reaction to the rise of the administrative state which resulted from the New Deal agenda. More specifically, the APA was intended to provide tools to more readily oversee agency action; *e.g.*, the APA provided procedural checks on administrative action and reinvigorated judicial review of agency action.

   Answer (D) is not correct. The phrase "the New Deal" refers to the ambitious agenda initiated by President Roosevelt in response to the collapse of the economy in the Great Depression. The agenda relied substantially on the need for a strong administrative state. The "New Dealers" created a host of new federal administrative agencies, expanded federal intervention in economic affairs, and laid the foundation for a national welfare state.

1.2.   Agency proceedings recognized by the APA include rule making, adjudication, and licensing. Section 551(12) of the APA provides that the phrase "agency proceeding" means an agency process as defined by §§ 551(5), (7) and (9). Section 551(5) provides that "rule making" is the agency process for formulating, amending or repeal ing a rule. Section 551(7) provides that "adjudication" is the agency process for the formulation of an order. And § 551(9) provides that "licensing" includes the agency process relating to licenses.

1.3.   **Answer (D) is correct** because the ESC is an agency; and the exemption determination involves an agency proceeding and agency action.

   Answer (A) is not correct because the ESC is an agency. The APA § 551(1) defines "agency" as "each authority of the Government of the United States, whether or not it is within or subject to review by another agency. . . ." The ESC is acting as an authority of the U.S. government. Additionally, the ESC does not fall within the specific exclusions set forth in § 551(1)(A)-(G).

Answer (B) is not correct. Even assuming that the ESC is an agency, certain agency action is exempt from APA procedural requirements. However, this statement is not accurate for two reasons. First, because it appears to be referring to the exemption from rulemaking requirements (*see* APA § 553(a)(2)) and, as is discussed in the following question, the ESC is not engaging in rulemaking. Second, although the BLM makes decisions relating to public property and thus might in some instances be exempt from the APA pursuant to § 553(a)(2), the determination by ESC relating to an exemption from the ESA prohibition does not fall within § 553(a)(2).

Answer (C) is not correct. Even assuming that the ESC is an agency, certain agency action is exempt from APA procedural requirements. However, this statement is not accurate because it also appears to be referring to an exemption from certain rulemaking requirements (*see* APA § 553(b)(2)(A)); and, as is discussed in the following question, the ESC is not engaging in rulemaking.

1.4.   **Answer (B) is correct.** APA § 551(6) defines "order" as "the whole or a part of a final disposition, whether affirmative [or] negative . . . , of an agency in a matter other than rule making but including licensing." Because the determination is not a "rule," the matter was not "rule making." *See* APA § 551(5). However, the determination may be characterized as licensing. APA § 551(9) defines "licensing" as the "agency process respecting the grant . . . denial . . . or conditioning of a license;" and § 551(8) defines "license" as the "whole or part of an agency permit, certificate . . . statutory exemption or other form of permission." The BLM was seeking a statutory exemption.

Answer (A) is not correct. APA § 551(4) defines a "rule" as "an agency statement of general or particular applicability and future effect designed to implement, interpret, or prescribe law or policy or describing the organization, procedure, or practice requirements of an agency. . . ." Here, the determination has a more present effect; and the determination is not designed to implement, interpret, or prescribe law or policy. The determination is better characterized as an application of the law to particular facts that has a present effect. The present effect of the determination is that the BLM's petition has been denied and BLM thus cannot proceed with its plans.

Answer (C) is not correct. The determination may accurately be characterized as "agency action" since APA § 551 (13) defines such action as "the whole or part of an agency rule, order, license . . . or the equivalent . . . thereof. . . ." However, "agency action" is not limited to actions that are final.

Answer (D) is not correct because APA § 551(11) defines "relief" as a favorable disposition and the ESC denied the BLM's petition for the exemption.

1.5.   **Answer (A) is an accurate statement.** A natural monopolist can increase its profits by restricting output and charging higher than competitive prices. Some agencies thus strive to ensure allocative efficiency by setting prices at levels that approximate those that would exist under competitive conditions.

Answer (B) is an accurate statement. Eliminating excessive competition is a debatable justification for administrative regulation. One historical example is the protection previously provided to the airline industry through minimum price regulation. The underlying rationale was that, if prices were allowed to be cut too low through excessive competition, most of the competing firms would go out of business; thereby allowing the few surviving firms to set prices artificially high.

Answer (C) is an accurate statement. For competitive markets to work well, consumers need information with which to evaluate competing products. However, information defects exist in many markets. Government regulation is sometimes designed to compensate for inadequate information or to lower the costs to consumers of obtaining adequate information.

Answer (D) is not an accurate statement. Some administrative regulation is grounded in non-economic justifications. For example, regulatory schemes such as the Social Security Act serve the purpose of redistributing resources from one group to another.

1.6.   **Answer (A) is an accurate statement.** Any agency charged with the authority to implement or enforce a regulatory scheme adopted by Congress has the authority to interpret the relevant statutory provisions. The key question is whether an agency has the power to engage in rule making or to enforce through adjudications. Thus, a grant of authority to promulgate substantive rules also will inherently authorize promulgation of interpretive rules.

Answer (B) is not an accurate statement. An agency has the power to promulgate substantive rules only if Congress has given it that power. The power to enforce a regulatory scheme may not carry with it the power to promulgate substantive rules. *Cf. National Petroleum Refiners Ass'n v. FTC*, 482 F.2d 672 (D.C. Cir. 1973).

Answer (C) is not an accurate statement. An agency can only promulgate rules within the scope of its delegated authority. Thus, one possible challenge to a rule promulgated by an agency is that it should be set aside on the grounds that the agency exceeded its authority. *See* APA § 706(2)(C).

Answer (D) is not an accurate statement. Even if an agency promulgates a rule within the scope of its delegated authority, that rule must comport with constitutional principles. Thus, one possible challenge to a rule promulgated by an agency is that it should be set aside on the grounds that the rule is contrary to a constitutional right, power, privilege, or immunity. *See* APA § 706(2)(B).

1.7.   **Answer (B) is an accurate statement.** In *Chenery II*, the Supreme Court noted, among other things, that an agency "may not have had sufficient experience with a particular problem to warrant rigidifying its tentative judgment into a hard and fast rule. Or the problem may be so specialized and varying in nature as to be impossible of capture within the boundaries of a general rule." *See SEC v. Chenery Corp.*, 332 U.S. 202–03. Thus, using adjudication to make new legal principles is viewed as more acceptable when addressing an emerging regulatory problem arising from variable industry practices.

Answer (A) is not an accurate statement. The Supreme Court has recognized that, although an agency should consider making law as much as possible through rule making, agencies must have flexibility to deal with regulatory problems in the manner they deem most appropriate. Certain situations and regulatory problems arguably are better addressed through ad hoc litigation and the decision whether to proceed through rule making or adjudication is vested primarily in the informed discretion of the agency. *See SEC v. Chenery Corp.*, 332 U.S. 194 (1947) (*Chenery II*).

Answer (C) is not an accurate statement. Although the decision whether to proceed through rule making or adjudication is vested primarily in the informed discretion of the agency, courts may set aside an order if the agency's use of adjudication amounts to an abuse of discretion. Imposing a substantial penalty or new liability on a regulated person or entity for violation of a legal principle not previously announced may, in some cases, warrant the setting aside of an agency order. *See, e.g., National Labor Relations Board v. Bell Aerospace Company Division of Textron Inc.*, 416 U.S. 267 (1974).

Answer (D) is not an accurate statement. Although the decision whether to proceed through rule making or adjudication is vested primarily in the informed discretion of the agency, courts may set aside an order if the agency's use of adjudication amounts to an abuse of discretion. Substantial reliance by a regulated person or entity on the agency's prior practice may, in some cases, warrant the setting aside of an agency order — especially if the order imposes a substantial penalty or new liability on a regulated person or entity for violation of a legal principle not previously announced. *See, e.g., National Labor Relations Board v. Bell Aerospace Company Division of Textron Inc.*, 416 U.S. 267 (1974).

1.8.   **Answer (A) is an accurate statement.** Congress may grant to agencies "subpoena power."

Answer (B) is not an accurate statement. Congress may grant to agencies the power to compel regulated entities to prepare and submit "reports" or other compilations of information.

Answer (C) is an accurate statement. Congress may grant to agencies the power to require regulated entities to permit inspection.

Answer (D) is not correct, since Answer (B) is an inaccurate statement.

1.9.   **Answer (C) is an accurate statement.** The Freedom of Information Act, § 552(a)(2), requires agencies to maintain indexes and to make available for inspection and copying not only final opinions and other orders made in the adjudication of cases, but also, statements of policy and interpretation not published in the Federal Register, administrative staff manuals and instructions to staff that affect the public, and copies of records which have been released to persons and which are likely to become the subject of subsequent requests.

Answer (A) is not an accurate statement. Agencies use the *Federal Register* to notify the public as to many agency actions; however, the *Federal Register* is published on a daily basis.

Answer (B) is not an accurate statement. The *Code of Federal Regulations* (CFR) contains all current agency regulations, not just those promulgated during the preceding twelve months.

Answer (D) is not an accurate statement. Section 552(a)(4)(i) authorizes agencies to promulgate, pursuant to notice and comment, regulations specifying the schedule of fees applicable to the processing of requests under the Freedom of Information Act. However, §552(a)(4)(iii) authorizes agencies to furnish copies of documents without charge or at a reduced charge if the disclosure of the information is in the public interest because it is likely to contribute significantly to public understanding of the operations or activities of government and is not primarily in the commercial interest of the

Rulemaking Procedures: Initiating Rule Making

2.1.   **Answer (B) represents one effective method** for prompting the agency to act. Agencies are aware of public perceptions about the appropriateness or inappropriateness of administrative regulation.

       Answer (C) represents one effective method for prompting the agency to act. Members of Congress can exert pressure or influence on administrative agencies.

       Answer (D) represents one effective method for prompting the agency to act. The argument to the agency combines concerns related to the agency's statutory mandate along with the industry's plight. Further, a formal petition for rulemaking requires the agency to at least consider whether a modification may be warranted. *See* APA § 553(e).

       Answer (A) is the least effective method for prompting the agency to act. All agency regulations tend to burden the persons and entities they regulate. Thus, an effective argument for modifying an agency rule should not focus primarily on the burden sustained by the industry. Rather, an effective argument would predominately focus on the agency's statutory mandate; here, protection of the national parks.

2.2.   In general, courts exercise caution in deciding whether to compel an agency to initiate rulemaking, by applying a "rule of reason" analysis. *See, e.g., Telecommunications Research & Action Center v. FCC*, 750 F.2d 70 (D.C. Cir. 1984). A statutory timetable supplies content for application of the rule of reason, but courts often construe such timetables as non-binding. *See, e.g., Action on Smoking and Health v. Department of Labor*, 100 F.3d 991, 994 (D.C. Cir. 1996) (noting that the statutory deadline was but one of several factors that a court should consider when deciding whether to intervene). Courts may decide not to enforce a statutory deadline when an agency can show that compliance is impossible; or when the effect of expediting action may have a negative impact on agency activities with a higher priority. *See, e.g., Telecommunications Research & Action Center v. FCC*, 750 F.2d 70 (D.C. Cir. 1984).

2.3.   The court likely would order the agency to promptly provide a timetable for the rulemaking and to provide period progress reports to the court. The court would also be likely to retain jurisdiction of the case until final agency action, in order to monitor and enforce the agency's compliance with its proposed timetable.

Exemptions from APA Notice & Comment Procedures

2.4.   **Answer (D) is the most accurate statement** for the reasons noted.

Answer (A) is not an accurate statement. Generally, notice of the agency's intent must be published in the Federal Register; but, exceptions exist.

Answer (B) is not an accurate statement. Agencies are not required to follow notice and comment for rule that constitute an interpretation of a statute or statements of agency policy; but, other exceptions also exist.

Answer (C) is not an accurate statement. Agencies are not required to follow notice and comment for rules that constitute an interpretation of a statute or an administrative rule; for statements of agency policy; or for a rule relating to internal agency procedure or practice. However, other exceptions also exist. Namely, rules for which the agency finds that "good cause" exists showing that notice and comment would be impractical, unnecessary, or contrary to the public interest. *See* APA 553(b)(2)(B). Additionally, the requirements of § 553 do not apply to military or foreign affairs functions; or to matters relating to agency management or personnel or to public property, loans, grants, benefits, or contracts. *See* APA § 553(a).

2.5.   Section 553(a) provides an exemption for matters involving a military or foreign affairs function of the United States and matters relating to agency management or personnel or to public property, loans, grants, benefits, or contracts. Section 553(b) provides an exemption for interpretive rules, general statements of policy, or rules of agency orga nization, procedure, or practice; and when the agency for good cause finds that it is impracticable, unnecessary or contrary to the public interest to engage and notice and its attendant public procedure. Thus, § 553(a) provides an exemption based on particu lar subject matter; whereas § 553(b) provides exemptions based on the type of rule. A key difference is that subsection (a) provides an exemption from all of § 553; whereas subsection (b) provides an exemption from subsection (b)'s notice requirement and, thereby, from subsection (c)'s comment requirement. Thus, for example, a matter exempted by subsection (a) includes an exemption for the agency relating to a petition for rulemaking. Importantly, neither (a) nor (b) exempts agency rules from the requirements of § 552.

2.6.   **Answer (C) is correct.** Agencies must use notice and comment to promulgate "sub stantive rules," i.e., rules that create rights or duties. For example, the key inquiry in deciding whether a rule falls within the exception for rules of "agency organization, procedure or practice" is whether the rule is essentially a "housekeeping measure" or a rule that alters merely the manner in which parties present themselves to the agency; or whether the rule affects, in a more substantive way, the rights and interests of regulated parties. *See, e.g., American Hosp. Ass'n v. Bowen*, 834 F.2d 1037 (D.C. Cir. 1987). The rules likely would be deemed "substantive" because they create new duties relating to private information. Further, statutory time limits on rulemaking ordinarily is an insufficient excuse for non-compliance with APA notice and comment proce dures. *See, e.g., Air Transportation Ass'n of Amer. v. Department of Transportation*, 900 F.2d 369 (D.C. Cir. 1990).

Answer (A) is incorrect because it likely would fall within section 553(b)'s good cause exception. The good cause exception requires an agency to find that the notice and comment procedures are "impracticable, unnecessary, or contrary to the public interest." A situation is "impractical" if the timely execution of agency functions would be impeded or if a safety measure must be put in place immediately. Certain pests, such as the Oriental fruit fly, create substantial risks to agriculture justifying immediate action.

Answer (B) is incorrect because it likely would fall within section 553(b)'s good cause exception. An oil spill likely creates risks of injury to health and the environment justifying immediate action.

Answer (D) is incorrect because it likely would fall within section 553(b)'s exception for rules of agency procedure or practice. The rules do not impose burdens on employers, or change the substantive standards used during inspections carried out by OSHA. The rules apply only internally, helping to ensure that OSHA uses its inspection resources effectively.

2.7.   **Answer (A) represents the most sound judicial response.** The good cause exception requires an agency to find that the notice and comment procedures are "impracticable, unnecessary, or contrary to the public interest." Courts narrowly construe the "good cause" exception. Here, for the reasons explained in the following answer selections, despite EPA's express finding of "good cause," the facts do not suggest a situation where the agency should be permitted to avoid notice and comment procedures. *See Utility Solid Waste Activities Group v. E.P.A.*, 236 F.3d 749 (D.C. Cir. 2001). Further, amendment of a legislative rule generally necessitates use of notice and comment procedures.

Answer (B) is incorrect. A situation is "impractical" only if the timely execution of agency functions would be impeded or if a safety measure must be put in place immediately. The amendment would seem to promote safety to health and the environment; but, the facts do not suggest any need for immediate action. In 1999, after notice and extensive commentary, EPA explained that the rule as originally promulgated would effectively prevent exposure to unreasonable risk.

Answer (C) is incorrect. The "unnecessary" exception is allowed for situations in which the rule is a routine, insignificant determination; one that is inconsequential to industry and the public. However, the amendment here is significant — especially to industries which are now subject to an increased regulatory burden. Under the amendment, the clean-up requirements are triggered by any spill of regulated, liquid PCBs since the ten micrograms per 100 centimeters trigger was, in essence, repealed.

Answer (D) is incorrect. The "public interest" exception is limited to situations in which the interest of the public would be defeated by any requirement of advance notice. For example, a situation where notice of a proposed rule would enable regulated persons to perhaps evade the rule; or where a safety measure must be put in place immediately. The facts do not present a situation where evasion of the new rule would be a concern; and, as noted above, the facts also do not suggest any need for immediate action.

2.8.   **Answer (A) is the most sound judicial response.** A rule is substantive (and thus not an interpretive rule) if, in the absence of a legislative rule, the legislative basis for the enforcement action is inadequate. *See American Mining Congress v. Mine Safety & Health Admin.*, 995 F.2d 1106 (D.C. Cir. 1993). That is, the question is whether the duty to use certain, specified diagnostic tests was imposed by Rule 501; or whether the PBI Guidelines create a new duty. The better analysis of the question is that Rule 501 creates only a duty to report, within ten days, the diagnosis of the PBIs. Rule 501 does not itself create a duty to use any particular tests to make the diagnosis. Further, the facts foreclose any argument by the CDC that the duty to use the tests specified in the PBI Guidelines is merely a clarification of the duty in Rule 501 because the Guidelines specify only those tests which would otherwise be required by the standard professional duty of care. Thus, because the duty to use the specified diagnostic tests is created by the PBI Guidelines, § 553(b)'s exemption for interpretive rules does not apply; and the CDC was required to use notice and comment procedures. Thus, because the duty is created by the PBI Guidelines, § 553(b)'s exemption for interpretive rules does not apply.

    Answer (B) is incorrect. One indicator that a rule is substantive is that the agency intended the rule to have the force and effect of law. *See American Mining Congress*, 995 F.2d 1106 (D.C. Cir. 1993). Thus, a finding that the CDC did not intend the Guidelines to have the force and effect of law would weigh in favor of the rule being interpretive; and would not support a finding that the law is invalid. Note, however, that the fact that CDC did not intend the Guidelines to have the force and effect of law is not determinative. Courts will look beyond the agency characterization to determine whether the law creates new rights or duties.

    Answer (C) is incorrect for the reason noted above.

    Answer (D) is incorrect. Although required (*see* § 552(a)), publication in the Federal Register is not a substitute for § 553's notice and comment procedures if the Guidelines constitute a substantive rule.

2.9.   **Answer (D) is the best answer** because Answers (B) and (C) both represent a sound judicial response. *See Hemp Industries Ass'n v. Drug Enforcement Admin.*, 333 F.3d 1082 (9th Cir. 2003).

    Answer (A) is incorrect for the reasons noted below.

    Answer (B) represents a sound judicial response. The Court of Appeals for the District of Columbia has recognized an exception to the general principle that interpretive rules are exempt from notice and comment. The doctrine allows a court to require an agency to use notice and comment for an interpretive rule if the interpretation changes a prior interpretation of a legislative rule promulgated by the agency. However, it is only appropriate to invoke the doctrine if the prior interpretation is sufficiently "authoritative" and if a substantial reliance interest exists. *See Alaska Professional Hunters Ass'n v. F.F.A.*, 177 F.3d 1030 (D.C. Cir. 1999). Here, the prior interpretation is sufficiently authoritative because it was provided by the Acting Administrator, published in the Federal Register and relied on by manufacturers for more than twenty years.

Answer (C) also represents a sound judicial response. A rule that is inconsistent with a prior legislative rule is not properly characterized as a mere interpretive rule. *See, e.g., American Mining Congress v. Mine Safety & Health Admin.*, 995 F.2d 1106 (D.C. Cir. 1993). Here, the 1968 rule seems to clearly ban only "synthetic equivalents" of THC.

2.10.   The doctrine hinges on the APA's definition of "rule making" to include the agency process of modifying a rule. *See* 5 U.S.C. § 551(5). According to the D.C. Circuit, the agency is, in essence, amending a rule in situations where the agency has previously provided a definitive interpretation of a rule and then later revises that interpretation.

See, e.g., Paralyzed Veterans of America v. D.C. Arena, 117 F.3d 579, 586 (D.C. Cir. 1997). Additionally, an agency interpretation of a statute cannot provide the same type of reliance as an agency interpretation of an agency rule — given the Court's clarification in the *Chevron* case that deference is not always given to an agency's interpretation of a statute. *See Chevron v. Natural Resources Defense Council, Inc.*, 467 U.S. 837 (U.S. 1984) (holding that, if a court is able to ascertain Congress' intention on the issue at hand, that intention is the law and must be given affect).

Notice & Comment Procedures

2.11.   **Answer (A) is correct.** Section 551(14) defines an ex parte communication as a communication, other than a status report, not on the public record with respect to which reasonable prior notice to all parties is not given. The communication with the IRS by the pharmaceutical industry representatives may fall within this definition if it is not made part of the rule making record. However, the APA's express prohibition on ex parte communications applies only in the context of formal rulemaking and adjudication. The APA does not expressly prohibit ex parte communications in informal rulemaking proceedings. Nonetheless, the U.S. Court of Appeals for the District of Columbia has cautioned agencies that rules may be set aside if undisclosed communications substantially diminish the "opportunity to comment" required by the APA. *See Sierra Club v. Costle*, 657 F.2d 298 (D.C. Cir. 1981). Thus, the IRS must consider whether a summary of the communication should be put in the public record.

Answer (B) is incorrect. Because the U.S. Court of Appeals for the District of Columbia has cautioned agencies that rules may be set aside if undisclosed communications substantially diminish the "opportunity to comment" required by the APA, the IRS must consider whether a summary of the communication should be put in the public record.

Answer (C) is incorrect. Section 551(14) defines an ex parte communication as a communication, other than a status report, not on the public record with respect to which reasonable prior notice to all parties is not given. However, the APA includes an express prohibition on ex parte communications only in the context of formal rulemaking and adjudication.

Answer (D) is incorrect. The U.S. Court of Appeals for the District of Columbia has held that, although the APA does not include an express prohibition on ex parte communications in informal rulemaking, such communications should be banned in a rule-making proceeding that involves "competing claims to a valuable privilege." However, the question involves a typical rulemaking proceeding, involving formulation of a standard for future application in a government program. The question does not involve a rulemaking that involves competing claims to a valuable privilege, such as an agency decision allocating "VHS channels" among cities. *See Sangamon Valley Television Corp. v. United States*, 269 F.2d 222 (D.C. Cir. 1959).

2.12.   **Answer (A) is correct.** Section § 553(b)(3) requires "notice" of a rulemaking to include "either the terms or substance of the proposed rule or a description of the subjects and issues involved." Courts have held that, when a final rule deviates from the proposed rule, the notice should be found adequate when the final rule represents "a logical out-growth" of the proposed notice and comments; or when the notice was sufficient to serve the policies underlying the notice requirement. *See, e.g., Chocolate Manufacturer's Ass'n v. Block*, 755 F.2d 1098 (4th Cir. 1985). Here, the notice alerted persons that an important issue involved in the rulemaking was whether expenses for herbal supplements should be allowed expenses.

Answer (B) is not correct. Section 553 (a) exempts from notice and comment requirements agency rulemaking that involves public benefits. However, the question involves a rule governing federal taxation of income.

Answer (C) is not correct. A final rule that reverses a position presented in the proposed rule arguably is a drastic deviation. However, the issue is whether interested parties were sufficiently put on notice of the issue underlying the position.

Answer (D) is not correct because courts have upheld final rules that reached a conclusion exactly opposite to a position in the proposed rule — as long as the notice sufficiently provided to interested parties a fair opportunity to comment on issues raised by the proposed rule or its description. *See, e.g., American Medical Ass'n v. United States*, 887 F.2d 760 (7th Cir. 1989).

2.13.   The phrase "non-legislative rules" refers to rules which administrative agencies may issue without following the APA's formal or informal rulemaking procedures. Congress, however, has ordinarily required publication of all rules — including rules that are exempt from rulemaking procedures. Section 552 (a)(1), part of the Freedom of Information Act, requires agencies to publish in the *Federal Register* rules of procedure, substantive rules of general applicability, and statements of general policy or interpretation of general application; as well as any amendments or revisions of such rules. *See also* § 553(d) (requiring publication of substantive rules 30 days prior to their effective date; and exempting certain other rules from the 30 day requirement, but not from the publication requirement).

2.14.   Section 553(c) requires a concise statement of the basis and purpose underlying a final rule. Congress did not intend for this provision to require an elaborate analysis of the rule or detailed discussion of the considerations underlying the rule. However, the standard of review used by courts when reviewing the substantive aspects of rules has resulted in agencies providing much more detailed and extensive explanations than what is technically required by the language of § 553(c). Supreme Court decisions have prompted agencies to draft contemporaneous explanations that (i) point to evidence in the rulemaking record supporting the rule, (ii) clarify the factors considered by the agency when deciding on the rule, and (iii) emphasize the logical connection between the evidence, findings of fact, and policy decisions. *See, e.g., Motor Vehicle Mfrs. Ass'n of United States v. State Farm Mutual Automobile Ins. Co.*, 463 U.S. 29 (1983).

Challenging a Legislative Interpretative Rule

2.15. The APA defines a "rule" as the "whole or a part of an agency statement of general or particular applicability and future affect designed to implement, interpret, or prescribe law or policy. . . ." *See* APA § 551(4). Rules promulgated pursuant to § 553's notice and comment procedures are referred to as "legislative rules." *See, e.g., American Mining Congress v. Mine Safety & Health Administration*, 995 F.2d 1106 (D.C. Cir. 1993) (explaining the factors to consider when determining whether an agency rule constitutes an invalid "legislative rule" because the agency failed to use notice and comment). In contrast, the phrase "non-legislative rule" is used to refer to rules for which notice and comment are not required; namely, interpretive rules, statements of agency policy, and rules of agency organization, procedure, or practice. *See* APA § 553(b)(A). A key dif ference between legislative and non-legislative rules is that non-legislative rules are not binding, on either the agency or the public.

2.16. Non-legislative rules are advantageous because they allow the agency to more quickly and efficiently provide information to the public as to the agency's views and intentions. Agencies can also use non-legislative rules to provide centralized guidance to, for example, local or regional offices, thereby regularizing agency action that affects the public. Moreover, although non-legislative rules are not "binding," regulated entities often comply with non-legislative rules. That is, although they are not binding in the sense that legislative rules are binding, regulated entities often comply because the rules reflect the agency's views regarding, for example, substantive aspects of statutes and future enforcement activities. On the other hand, because non-legislative rules are crafted without public input, they may fail to address a particular interest or concern; or otherwise fall short of the best regulatory response. Additionally, regulated entities which believe that a rule is unwise or illegal face a dilemma: they must either comply or risk having to challenge the rule in an enforcement proceeding. Further, even a complying entity may find itself subject to an enforcement proceeding if the agency changes its mind. Although the advantages of non-legislative rules generally inure to the benefit of agencies, an agency may nonetheless elect to use notice and comment for an interpretive rule because the agency wants input from the regulated industry — for policy and political reasons.

2.17. **Answer (B) is the most accurate statement.** The Court in *Chevron* created a two-step analysis. In the first step, the court asks whether there is clear congressional intent regarding the precise issue before the court. "If the intent of Congress is clear, that is the end of the matter. . . ." *Chevron v. Natural Resources Defense Council, Inc.*, 467 U.S. 837 (1984). In footnote 9, the Court clarified that, "[i]f a court, employing traditional tools of statutory construction, ascertains that Congress had an intention on the precise question at issue, that intention is the law and must be given effect." *Id.* at 843 n.9. As in the question, tools of statutory construction often support differing interpretations.

That does not mean, however, that a court must shift to step-two. The question is simply whether a court can find congressional intent. Here, it is likely that the Supreme Court would find congressional intent. Congress defined "disability" and the Court, engaging in statutory interpretation, would decide which interpretation is more sound.

Answer (A) is not an accurate statement. Although the APA directs courts to decide all relevant questions of law, the Supreme Court historically, and more explicitly in the *Chevron* case, has recognized that in some cases it may be appropriate to defer to an executive agency's construction of a statutory scheme it is entrusted to administer. *See Chevron v. Natural Resources Defense Council, Inc.*, 467 U.S. 837 (1984).

Answer (C) is not an accurate statement. Congress was not silent on the precise issue because Congress defined "disability" and likely intended one of the two interpretations presented in the question.

Answer (D) is not an accurate statement. As noted, tools of statutory construction often support differing interpretations. That does not mean, however, that the statute is "ambiguous" as that term was used by the Court in *Chevron*. The question is whether a court can find congressional intent. Here, it is likely that the Supreme Court would find congressional intent. Congress defined "disability" and the Court would decide which interpretation is more sound. *Chevron v. Natural Resources Defense Council, Inc.*, 467 U.S. 837 (1984).

2.18. **Answer (B) is an accurate statement.** The essence of *Chevron* deference is that, sometimes, it is apparent that Congress intended to delegate to the agency the authority to elucidate, through regulation, a specific provision of the statutory scheme the agency has been entrusted to administer. *Chevron v. Natural Resources Defense Council, Inc.*, 467 U.S. 837 (1984).

Answer (A) is not an accurate statement. As noted, tools of statutory construction often support differing interpretations. That does not mean, however, that the statute is "ambiguous" as that term was used by the Court in *Chevron*. The question is whether a court can find congressional intent. *Chevron v. Natural Resources Defense Council, Inc.*, 467 U.S. 837 (1984).

Answer (C) is not an accurate statement. As noted, a court should defer only when it has determined that Congress did not have an intent regarding the issue; i.e., when Congress has explicitly or implicitly left a gap for the agency to fill. That is not the same as when a statute is ambiguous. The Court in *Chevron* explained that deference in that type of circumstance is appropriate because the task often involves reconciling conflicting policies or depends on more than ordinary knowledge respecting matters delegated to agency expertise. But, interpretation of an ambiguous provision sometimes also arguably involves such considerations. *Chevron v. Natural Resources Defense Council, Inc.*, 467 U.S. 837 (1984).

Answer (D) is not an accurate statement for the reasons provided above.

2.19.   Agencies are more likely to prevail at step-two of the *Chevron* analysis. At step-one, agencies are not accorded any deference. At step-one, courts are simply engaging in statutory interpretation — i.e., using tools of statutory interpretation to determine whether Congress had an intention on the issue at hand. *See, e.g., Chevron v. Natural Resources Defense Council, Inc.*, 467 U.S. 837, 843 n. 9 (1984). A court proceeds to step-two of the analysis only if the court determines that Congress did not have an intention as to that issue. And, at step-two, courts are deferential to the agency; i.e., courts will uphold the agency's interpretative rule if the rule is reasonable or permissible.

2.20   The Court in *Mead* reaffirmed the importance of, and the authority to, tailor the use of judicial deference to agency action. ("The Court's choice has been to tailor deference to variety.") The Court stated that *Chevron* was simply a case recognizing the appropriateness of according broad deference even without an express authorization by Congress to fill a specific statutory gap. Further, the Court made clear that, because of the infinite variety of ways in which an agency may implement a statute, the *Skidmore* formulation remains viable. Thus, the measure of judicial deference may vary, depending on the agency's care; its consistency, formality, and relative expertise; and on the persuasiveness of the agency's position. Specifically regarding use of the *Chevron* approach to reviewing agency action, the Court in *Mead* stated that even without an express delegation of specific interpretive authority, other circumstances may make it apparent that Congress expected that the agency would be able to speak with the force of law when addressing ambiguities or filling gaps. The Court in *Gonzales* then clarified the type of circumstances triggering the *Chevron* approach. The *Gonzales* Court stated that *Chevron* deference is warranted only when it appears that Congress delegated authority to the agency generally to make rules carrying the force of law, and that the agency interpretation claiming deference was promulgated in the exercise of that authority.

Challenging the Substantive Aspects of a Rule

2.21.   **Answer (C) represents a sound judicial response.** The Supreme Court has explained that a rule would be arbitrary and capricious if, among other things, the agency relied on factors which Congress did not intend for it to consider. *See, e.g., Motor Vehicle Mfrs. Ass'n of United States v. State Farm Mutual Automobile Ins. Co.*, 463 U.S. 29 (1983). The statement of basis and purpose suggests that the IRS perhaps considered factors such as safety and efficacy, but did not give more weight to them than the factors which Congress intended — namely, considerations of fairness and reasonableness from a tax perspective.

Answer (A) is not a sound judicial response because § 706(2)(E)'s "substantial evidence" standard of review applies to agency determinations made in formal rulemaking or formal adjudications, not those made in informal rulemaking.

Answer (B) is not a sound judicial response because, although the correct standard of review is § 706(2)(A)'s arbitrary and capricious standard, a court using that standard scrutinizes the rule for more than a plausible basis for the policy decision.

Answer (D) is not a sound judicial response. In *State Farm*, the Court explained that the agency must articulate a satisfactory explanation for its actions, including a rational connection between the facts found and the choice made. *Motor Vehicle Mfrs. Ass'n of United States v. State Farm Mutual Automobile Ins. Co.*, 463 U.S. 29 (1983). Here, the agency supplied a connection; in both situations taxpayers are using income to address health conditions. Although not all would agree with the policy choice, it is not implausible given the IRS's expertise in considering fairness of taxation issues.

2.22.   **Answer (D) is the best answer.** For the reasons provided above, both Answers (A) and (B) represent sound judicial responses.

Answer (A) represents a sound judicial response because, although § 706(2)(E) does not normally apply to informal rulemaking, Congress has imposed the substantial evidence standard through the statute.

Answer (B) also represents a sound judicial response. In the *State Farm* case, the Court explained that a rule would be arbitrary and capricious if, among other things, the agency relied on factors which Congress did not intend for it to consider. *Motor Vehicle Mfrs. Ass'n of United States v. State Farm Mutual Automobile Ins. Co.*, 463 U.S. 29 (1983). The statement of basis and purpose suggests that the IRS perhaps considered factors such as safety and efficacy, but did not give more weight to them than the factors which Congress intended — namely, considerations of fairness and reasonableness from a tax perspective.

Answer (C) is not a sound judicial response. In *State Farm*, the Court explained that the agency must articulate a satisfactory explanation for its actions, including a rational connection between the facts found and the choice made. *Motor Vehicle Mfrs. Ass'n of United States v. State Farm Mutual Automobile Ins. Co.*, 463 U.S. 29 (1983). Here, the agency supplied a connection; in both situations taxpayers are using income to address health conditions. Although not all would agree with the policy choice, it is not implausible given the IRS's expertise in considering fairness of taxation issues.

2.23.   Under § 706, courts may set aside "agency action, findings, and conclusions" if the court finds them to be

(A)   arbitrary, capricious, or an abuse of discretion;

(B)   contrary to a constitutional right, power, privilege, or immunity;

(C)   inconsistent with statutory mandates;

(D) in violation of required procedure;

(E) unsupported by substantial evidence in a case subject to formal rule making procedures; or

(F) unwarranted by the facts — in a case where the facts may be tried do novo by the reviewing court.

See APA § 706(2).

Courts are non-deferential when making a decision under subsections (B), (C), (D), or (F). That is, when deciding whether a rule should be set aside for the reasons designated in (B), (C), (D), or (F), the court decides the matter "de novo" — without giving any deference to the agency. This is because the reasons set forth in (B), (C), and (D) require an assessment of whether the agency has violated the law. In those cases no deference is appropriate. Subsection (F) does not involve a legal issue; but, is expressly limited to rare cases in which the reviewing court holds a de novo trial to determine the relevant facts. In contrast, the reasons set forth in (A) & (E) require a court to proceed with deference to the agency's actions.

2.24. **Answer (A) is an accurate statement.** Although both are similar in that the agency rule will be upheld unless it is arbitrary, hard look review is less deferential because it provides a vehicle for the court to set aside agency action even if the rule is reasonable. That is, the court scrutinizes the explanation and may set the rule aside if the explanation is inadequate. *See Motor Vehicle Mfrs. Ass'n of United States v. State Farm Mutual Automobile Ins. Co.,* 463 U.S. 29 (1983).

Answer (B) is not an accurate statement. Although step-one of *Chevron v. Natural Resources Defense Council, Inc.,* 467 U.S. 837 (1984), may be characterized as de novo, because the court determines for itself whether Congress has indicated its intent regarding the statutory issue; step-two of *Chevron* clearly accords deference to agency determinations. Further, "hard look" review is arbitrary and capricious review — and is, therefore, deferential. *Id.*

Answer (C) is not an accurate statement. Although both are deferential, hard look review is less deferential because it provides a vehicle for the court to set aside agency action even if the rule is reasonable. That is, the court scrutinizes the explanation and may set the rule aside if the explanation is inadequate.

Answer (D) is not an accurate statement. The analysis modeled by the Court in *Chevron* is distinct from the analysis modeled by the Court in *Motor Vehicle Mfrs. Ass'n of United States v. State Farm Mutual Automobile Ins. Co.,* 463 U.S. 29 (1983).

2.25. **Answer (C) is correct.** This is not a valid concern. In hard look review, a court is not permitted to impose a heightened evidentiary standard to factual findings. Rather, hard look review allows a court to focus on the explanation and the rational connection between facts found and the policy choice made by the agency.

Answer (A) is incorrect. This is a valid concern because allowing courts to scrutinize the adequacy of an agency's explanation of a rule opens the door for courts to set aside an agency rule due to a bias, and to justify doing so by pointing to minimal gaps in the agency explanation.

Answer (B) is incorrect. This is a valid concern. Hard look review does, in essence, impose a procedural requirement: the requirement to more fully articulate an explanation for the rule which demonstrates that the agency carefully considered whether the rule flows logically from the findings of fact. *See Vermont Yankee Nuclear Power Corp. v. Natural Resources Defense Council, Inc.*, 435 U.S. 579 (1978).

Answer (D) is incorrect. This is a valid concern. Hard look review does, in essence, impose an additional procedural requirement: the requirement to more fully articulate an explanation for the rule which demonstrates that the agency carefully considered whether the rule flows logically from the findings of fact. As noted, however, this is arguably inconsistent with *Vermont Yankee Nuclear Power Corp. v. Natural Resources Defense Council, Inc.*, 435 U.S. 579 (1978).

2.26. A court will remand the rule back to agency and, in essence, allow the agency an opportunity to cure the defect. *See, e.g., SEC v. Chenery Corp*, 318 U.S. 80 (1943) (explaining that a reviewing court may only review the justification made by the agency, and may not supply its own).

Beyond the APA: Other Mandated Procedural Requirements for Rulemaking

2.27. **Answer (C) is an accurate statement.** The Act requires a Regulatory Flexibility Analysis when a rule may have a significant economic impact on a substantial number of small businesses, organizations, or governments.

Answer (A) is not an accurate statement. The Paperwork Reduction Act is concerned with unnecessary federal recordkeeping and reporting requirements.

Answer (B) is not an accurate statement. A series of executive orders, such as Executive Order 12,291 and Executive Order 12,866, are the primary sources of the need for cost/benefit analyses by federal agencies for major rules or significant agency action.

Answer (D) is not an accurate statement. The Unfunded Mandates Reform Act of 1995 is concerned with federal mandates requiring significant expenditures by state, local, or tribal governments or by the private sector.

2.28. **Answer (A) is an accurate statement.** *See* 5 U.S.C. § 611(a)(4)(A) & (B).

Answer (B) is not an accurate statement. Courts are not required to remand the rule. *See* 5 U.S.C. § 611(a)(4)(A) & (B).

Answer (C) is not an accurate statement. The Act provides that, in an action for judicial review of a rule, the Regulatory Flexibility Analysis shall become a part of the "entire record of agency action in connection with such review." *See* 5 U.S.C. § 611(b). Thus, when applying the arbitrary and capricious standard of review (or the substantial evidence standard of review if required by statute), courts will be able to consider the substance of the Regulatory Flexibility Analysis.

Answer (D) is not an accurate statement. The Act authorizes courts to review claims of agency noncompliance; and, if found, authorizes courts to remand the rule or to defer enforcement of the rule. *See* 5 U.S.C. § 611(a)(4)(A) & (B).

2.29.   **Answer (A) is not an accurate statement.** Section 10 provides that the Order is intended only to improve internal management, and that the Order does not create any right or benefit, substantive or procedural, enforceable at law or equity by a party against the United States or its agencies or instrumentalities, or its officers or employees.

   Answers (B), (C), and (D) are not accurate statements for the reason noted above.

2.30.   Several arguments support the view that the additional requirements enhance rulemaking. Centralized coordination helps ensure more efficient rulemaking across the whole of the federal government; and additional assessments, such as cost versus benefit or costs imposed on small businesses, should help ensure a "better" or "more effective" regulatory scheme. On the other hand, an increase in procedural requirements arguably makes rulemaking as to individual regulatory actions less efficient. Additional assessments make it more costly to promulgate individual rules and slow down the rulemaking process — and thus have been blamed, in part, for the stagnation of rulemaking.

2.31.   **Answer (C) is an accurate statement.** *See* 5 U.S.C. § 565(a) & § 566(a).

   Answer (A) is not an accurate statement. Section 6(a) of Executive Order 12,866 directs agencies to explore and "where appropriate" use consensual methods of rulemaking, including negotiated rulemaking.

   Answer (B) is not an accurate statement. Section 563 authorizes an agency to make an initial determination as to whether a negotiated rulemaking committee can adequately represent the interests affected and whether it is feasible and appropriate to use negotiated rulemaking procedures. However, before proceeding, § 564 and § 565 require the agency to publish in the *Federal Register* information about its proposal to use negotiated rulemaking and to solicit and consider comments on the proposal to establish a committee.

   Answer (D) is not an accurate statement. The negotiated rulemaking procedures contemplate that the committee's consensus conclusions constitute a proposed rule. *See* 5 U.S.C. § 562(7) and § 566 (a) & (f). Accordingly, the agency must then proceed with informal notice and comment procedures.

3.1.   Section 551(7) of the APA defines "adjudication" as an "agency process for the formula tion of an order." Section 551(6) defines "order" as the "whole or part of a final disposition . . . of an agency in a matter other than rule making but including licensing." Section 551(5) defines "rulemaking" as the "agency process for formulating, amending, or repeal ing a rule." A "rule" is defined by § 551(4) as "the whole or part of an agency statement of general . . . applicability and future affect. . . ." An "adjudication" then, is the agency process for formulating a decision of "particular" applicability and "present" effect. Stated another way, agency rulemaking is more akin to legislation enacted by a legis lature; whereas adjudication is more akin to a judgment imposed by a court. That is, in rulemaking an agency addresses a problem by crafting a rule that will affect all regu lated entities and that takes affect only after its promulgation and publication. In contrast, adjudication permits an agency to address a problem by crafting what is, in essence, a rule that affects only specific entities (those before the agency in the administrative pro ceeding); and that can, in some instances, affect them even if the agency position was not previously known.

3.2.   Most of the procedures set out in the APA that apply to adjudications are not required for the vast majority of agency adjudications. APA § 554 and § 556 apply only to cases of adjudication "required by statute to be determined on the record after opportunity for an agency hearing. . . ." The Supreme Court has not decided what this language means in the adjudication context; but, in the rulemaking context the Court held that formal APA requirements would be triggered only upon clear congressional intent that the determination be based on a closed record. *See, e.g., U.S. v. Florida Coast Railroad Co.*, 410 U.S. 224 (1973). A *Chevron* analysis would likely lead to the same result in the adjudication context. Additionally, it is well recognized that the full collection of APA's procedural entitlements are not necessary — even if due process is triggered. Due process considerations often demand only limited procedural protections. *Chevron v. Natural Resources Defense Council, Inc.*, 467 U.S. 837 (1984).

3.3.   **Answer (B) reflects the most sound judicial response.** Whether a congressional requirement of a "hearing" triggers the APA protections is a matter of statutory interpretation, which in turn is a matter of congressional intent. Further, *Chevron* deference to the agency's interpretation is not triggered unless the reviewing court cannot ascertain, using traditional tool of statutory interpretation, congressional intent on the issue. *Chevron v. Natural Resources Defense Council, Inc.*, 467 U.S. 837 (1984).

        Answer (A) is not the most sound judicial response. Section 554(a) states that the for mal APA adjudication requirements apply in "every case of adjudication required by statute to be determined on the record after opportunity for an agency hearing. . . ." However, it was in the rulemaking context — not the adjudication context — that the Supreme Court held that formal APA requirements would be triggered only upon clear congressional intent that the determination be based on a closed record. *See, e.g., U.S. v. Florida Coast Railroad Co.*, 410 U.S. 224 (1973).

Answer (C) is not the most sound judicial response. The Supreme Court decisions in the rulemaking context, noted above, would not support this presumption. It is true that the Court's holding in the rulemaking context was based on the sentiment that trial-like procedures are rarely necessary for fairness in rulemaking, given its more legislative character; and, thus, that adjudications may require greater procedural protections. However, it is also well recognized that the full collection of APA's procedural entitlements are not necessary in all adjudications — even if due process is triggered. Due process considerations often demand only limited procedural protections.

Answer (D) is not the most sound judicial response. Although the issue presents a question of statutory interpretation, *Chevron* deference to the agency interpretation is not triggered unless the reviewing court cannot ascertain, using traditional tool of statutory interpretation, congressional intent on the issue. *Chevron v. Natural Resources Defense Council, Inc.*, 467 U.S. 837 (1984).

3.4.   **Answer (A) is an accurate statement.** Although the generally understood principle is that an APA adjudication must be based entirely on the exclusive record referred to in § 556(e), § 556(e) recognizes that an ALJ may take "official notice of a material fact not appearing in the record" — as long as the opposing party is afforded the opportunity, upon request, to show the contrary. Basic information concerning mortality rates may be found to constitute the type of material of which an ALJ may take "official notice."

Answer (B) is not an accurate statement because § 556(d) provides that the "proponent of a rule or order has the burden of proof," and the Supreme Court has held that this language includes the concept of burden of persuasion. *See Director, Office of Workers' Compensation Programs, Dept. of Labor v. Greenwich Collieries*, 512 U.S. 267 (1994). In this case, Tony is the proponent of the order because it is Tony who is seeking an order granting him Medicare benefits. Thus, Tony has the burden of persuasion on the issue of reasonable and necessary.

Answer (C) is not an accurate statement because the process describes the ALJ decision as one which may be appealed to the agency (the Appeals Council). Under § 557(b), a determination by the presiding officer is an "initial decision" and not a "recommended decision" unless the agency requires the ALJ to certify the entire record to the agency for decision.

Answer (D) is not an accurate statement because § 556(d) permits the agency to adopt procedures for the submission of all or part of the evidence in written form if the adjudication involves a claim for money or benefits — if the party will not be prejudiced. Tony's claim is for benefits under the Medicare program. Further, Tony likely would not be prejudiced because the evidence which would be provided by Tony's oncologists can be presented via affidavits.

3.5. **Answer (A) is an accurate statement.** ALJ are employees of the agencies for whom they work and they must apply interpretations and policy determinations of the agency.

Answer (B) is not an accurate statement for the reason stated above.

Answer (C) is not an accurate statement. Physician opinions presented in the form of affidavits may constitute sufficient evidence to support an agency determination. Because Tony has the right to subpoena witnesses to preserve his right to cross-examine, no absolute rule precludes an ALJ from relying on evidence in the form of affidavits. The agency cannot, however, base its decision on opinions of oncologists submitted by way of affidavits after the hearing, without re-opening the hearing or otherwise giving Tony an opportunity to rebut the evidence. *Richardson v. Perales*, 402 U.S. 389 (1971).

Answer (D) is incorrect because Answer (A) is an accurate statement.

3.6. **Answer (D) is an accurate statement** for the reasons noted above. Further, § 557(c) requires agencies to allow parties to submit for consideration proposed findings and conclusions, and reasons supporting those findings and conclusions — before a decision on agency review of the decision of subordinate employees.

Answer (A) is not an accurate statement. The substantial evidence standard of § 706(2)(E) applies when courts are reviewing agency orders made pursuant to formal, APA procedures. Section 557(b) directs that, "on appeal or review of the initial decision, the agency has all the powers which it would have in making the initial decision." This means that the agency's Appeal Council may decide the case without deferring to the ALJ's determination.

Answer (B) is not an accurate statement. The arbitrary and capricious standard of § 706(2)(A) applies when courts are reviewing rule or orders promulgated pursuant to informal APA procedures. And, as noted, § 557(b) directs that, "on appeal or review of the initial decision, the agency has all the powers which it would have in making the initial decision." This means that the agency's Appeal Council may decide the case without deferring to the ALJ's determination.

Answer (C) is not an accurate statement. Section 557(b) directs that, "on appeal or review of the initial decision, the agency has all the powers which it would have in making the initial decision." Although this means that the appeal is conducted, in essence, de novo, the review generally does not include additional taking of evidence.

3.7. **Answer (C) is an accurate statement** for the reason noted above.

Answer (A) is not an accurate statement. Although § 706(2) authorizes courts only to "set aside" agency action, findings, or conclusions, the statute specifically authorizing judicial review in the question also allows the court "to modify or reverse" the decision of the agency, with or without remanding the cause for a rehearing.

Answer (B) is not an accurate statement because the statute states that findings of fact, if supported by substantial evidence, shall be conclusive. Thus, the statutory authorization to modify or reverse the decision of the agency, with or without remanding the cause for a rehearing, cannot be based upon factual findings unless those facts were unsupported by substantial evidence. And, as is discussed *infra*, the substantial evidence standard is distinct from the arbitrary and capricious standard.

Answer (D) is incorrect because Answer (C) is an accurate statement.

3.8.   **Answer (B) is an accurate statement** for the reasons noted above.

Answer (A) is not an accurate statement. It is partially correct because the memorandum itself is not a "prohibited" ex parte communication. Section 557(d)(1) prohibits, in cases where formal APA procedures apply, ex parte communications relevant to the merits of the proceeding, but only if by persons outside the agency to an agency employee involved in the decisional process, or vice versa. Here, the communication is from a person within the CMM. However, although not a prohibited communication, it is still an ex parte communication if it is not made part of the record. *See* § 551(14). Moreover, § 556(e) indicates that formal procedures require an "exclusive record for decision," and thus, indicates that Congress intended that any communication or other evidence considered by the decision maker would be made a part of the public record.

Answer (C) is not an accurate statement. The communication is not a "prohibited" ex parte communication. Further, the APA does not require that prohibited ex parte communications be disregarded. Rather § 557(d)(1)(C) would require the decision maker to place the communication on the public record and to consider whether the interests of justice require some additional sanction.

Answer (D) is not an accurate statement, because the communication is not a "prohibited" ex parte communication.

3.9.   **Answer (C) is an accurate statement** for the reasons noted below.

Answer (A) is not an accurate statement. Although the memorandum itself is not a "prohibited" ex parte communication, the letter from private insurers likely is a prohibited communication. Section 557(d)(1) prohibits ex parte communications relevant to the merits of the proceeding if made by persons outside the agency, or if the person out-side the agency knowingly caused the communication to be made to an agency employee involved in the decisional process. Here, the letter is from persons outside the agency, and, at least arguably, the insurers knowingly caused the communication to be made to the decision maker. The communication is also relevant to the merits of the proceding — namely, whether to consider HDC/BMT experimental and thus ineligible for Medicare coverage.

Answer (B) is only a partially accurate statement. A reasonable argument exists that the letter from the private insurers constitutes a "prohibited" ex parte communication. However, the APA does not require that prohibited ex parte communications be disregarded. Rather § 557(d)(1)(C) would require the decision maker to place the communication on the public record and to consider whether the interests of justice require some additional sanction.

Answer (D) is incorrect because Answer (C) is an accurate statement.

3.10.   **Answer (A) is the most sound judicial response.** Courts have held that improper ex parte communications, even when undisclosed during agency proceedings, do not necessarily void an agency decision. *See, e.g., Professional Air Traffic Controllers Organization v. Federal Labor Relations Authority*, 685 F.2d 547 (D.C. Cir. 1982). Rather, courts consider whether the agency decision making process was "irrevocably tainted so as to make the ultimate judgment of the agency unfair, either to an innocent party or to the public interest." *Id.* Courts consider a number of factors in making this determination: the gravity of the communication; whether the party making or causing the communication benefited from the agency judgment; whether the communication presented information that was unknown to opposing parties; and whether voiding the judgment would serve any useful purpose.

Answer (B) is not the most sound judicial response for the reasons noted above.

Answer (C) is not the most sound judicial response. The fact that the letter was not made part of the record is not, alone, sufficient to warrant a finding that the process of decision making was irrevocably tainted.

Answer (D) is incorrect, because Answer (A) reflects a sound judicial response.

3.11.   The communication is prohibited by the APA. Section 554(d) prohibits any participa tion in the ALJ decision making process, by an employee or agent of the agency who engaged in the performance of investigative or prosecuting functions in the case before the ALJ or in a factually related case. Unlike § 557(d), which includes an administrative remedy for violation of the prohibition on ex parte communications in formal agency adjudications, § 554(d) does not address the proper remedy at the administrative level. Upon judicial review, however, courts treat violations of § 554 similarly to violations of the § 557 prohibition. A violation of § 554 does not necessarily void the agency judg ment, but courts will carefully scrutinize for fairness concerns.

3.12.   When an agency adjudication must be conducted pursuant to the "formal procedures," § 556 requires that there be a "presiding" officer or employee. Section 556 provides that an administrative law judge may preside at the taking of evidence; administrative law judges generally are employees of the agency. Section 556(c) authorizes presiding employees to function much like judges. They are authorized to administer oaths; issue subpoenas; rule on offers of proof and receive relevant evidence; take or order deposi tions; regulate the course of the hearing; rule on procedural requests or similar matters; make or recommend decisions; hold settlement conferences and compel attendance; and encourage alternative dispute resolution. Section 556 also provides that the presiding employee must act in an impartial manner.

3.13.   The APA does not specify requirements applicable solely to informal adjudication. However, the minimal requirements of § 555 are applicable to all agency proceedings. Those procedures include: the right in any proceeding to be represented by counsel; the right of interested persons to appear before an agency in any proceeding "so far as the orderly conduct or public business permits; the right to have an agency conclude a matter presented to the agency within a "reasonable time"; the right to retain or obtain copies of materials required to be submitted to an agency; the right to utilize agency subpoena power upon a showing of general relevance and reasonable scope of the evidence sought; and the right to receive prompt notice of a denial of a request, application, or petition, as well as a brief statement of the grounds for a denial.

3.14.   Whether ALJs can serve with independence and neutrality is a valid concern given that ALJs are employees of the agency for which they serve as judges (*see* 5 U.S.C. § 3105), and that the agency generally is a party in a proceeding before the ALJ. Accordingly, Congress has adopted important provisions to mitigate that concern. Foremost, agencies are not allowed to rate, evaluate, discipline, reward, punish, or remove ALJs who work for them; rather, adverse personnel actions can only be made by the Merit Systems Protection Board after a formal APA adjudication. *See* 5 U.S.C. § 7521. Additionally, the APA includes specific provisions which help ensure independence and neutrality. For example, with certain exceptions, the APA prohibits an agency employee engaged in investigation or prosecution of a case from participating or advising in the ALJ's deci sion or recommended decision. *See* 5 U.S.C. § 554(d). Further, the APA provides that ALJs are subject to disqualification for personal bias or other reason from hearing a case. *See* 5 U.S.C. § 556(b).

3.15.   Appeals within an agency are different in nature from judicial appellate review of a trial court. The APA provides that the agency "has all the powers which it would have in making the initial decision." *See* APA § 557(b). Thus, when an ALJ decision is appealed, the appeals board or agency head decides the case de novo.

3.16.   **Answer (C) is an accurate statement.** Although for a number of years the Supreme Court utilized a "rights/privilege" distinction which would preclude application of the due process clause to agency actions affecting government largesse, the Court in *Goldberg v. Kelly* abandoned that distinction. *See* 397 U.S. 254 (1970). Today, due process protections are triggered by agency actions which adversely affect legitimate entitlements to government benefits. In *Goldberg*, the Court specifically held that termination of welfare benefits trigger due process protections. *Id.*

Answer (A) is not an accurate statement. Due process protections are triggered by agency actions that constitute a deprivation of property or liberty interests. Adjudications, more often than rulemaking, may result in a deprivation of a protected interest. However, not all adverse agency adjudications trigger due process rights and, thus, an initial issue is always whether the due process clause applies at all. *See, e.g., Goldberg v. Kelly,* 397 U.S. 254 (1970).

Answer (B) is not an accurate statement. Rulemaking rarely triggers the protection of the due process clause. Agency rulemaking is not based on individualized grounds and, generally, is based on legislative rather than adjudicative facts. Legislative facts are general facts which bear on the subject of the rulemaking. Adjudicative facts concern particular persons and questions such as who did what, when, where, why, and how, etc. *Compare Londoner v. Denver*, 210 U.S. 373 (1908), *with Bi-Metallic Investment Co. v. State Board of Equalization*, 239 U.S. 441 (1915).

Answer (D) is incorrect for the reasons noted above.

3.17. **Answer (B) is the most sound judicial response.** Because the University did not make any finding relating to Susan's name, reputation, honor, or integrity, this is not a case where the State has imposed a stigma that would foreclose Susan's freedom to obtain other employment opportunities. *See Board of Regents v. Roth*, 408 U.S. 564 (1972).

Answer (A) is not a sound judicial response. The facts do not raise any issue relating to jurisdiction to review the decision.

Answer (C) is not a sound judicial response. Because the University did not make any finding relating to Susan's name, reputation, honor, or integrity, this is not a case where the State has imposed a stigma that would foreclose Susan's freedom to obtain other employment opportunities. *See Board of Regents v. Roth*, 408 U.S. 564 (1972).

Answer (D) is not a sound judicial response. Because of the terms of Susan's employment contract, the determination did not deprive her of a legitimate property interest. Further, the facts do not suggest the existence of any university policies which could support Susan's claim of a property interest.

3.18. The idea that "stigma" resulting from government action could give rise to due process rights arose from language use by the Supreme Court in *Board of Regents v. Roth*, 408 U.S. (1972). In *Roth*, the Court explained that liberty interests "denote[ ] not merely free dom from bodily restraint but also the right of the individual to contract, to engage in any of the common occupations of life, to acquire useful knowledge . . . and generally to enjoy those privileges long recognized . . . as essential to the orderly pursuit of hap piness by free men." *Id.* However, the Court in *Roth* found that an assistant professor did not have a protectable liberty interest triggering due process rights because "the state, in declining to rehire [him], did not make any charge against him that might seri ously damage his standing and association in his community." *Id.* The Court stated that where "a person's good name, reputation, honor, or integrity is at stake because of what the government is doing to him, notice and an opportunity to be heard are essential." *Id.* The Court later clarified that stigma alone was insufficient to trigger due process rights. In *Paul v. Davis*, 424 U.S. 693 (1976), the Court explained that "reputation alone, apart from some more tangible interests such as employment, is [n]either 'liberty' or 'property' by itself sufficient to invoke the procedural protection of the Due Process Clause." The analysis in *Paul* has been described as the "stigma-plus" test. That is, in order to trigger due process protections, the government action must do more than simply harm a person's reputation; the action must also subject the individual to some other significant loss, such as the loss of a job or an invasion of privacy.

3.19. **Answer (D) is the most accurate statement.** This answer consists of an argument more in-line with the Supreme Court's decisions to the effect that "stigma-plus" is essential to trigger due process. That is, that the government action must both harm the person's reputation and subject the person to some other loss: loss of a government privilege such as a job; loss of a legal right such as the right to purchase alcohol; or loss of another liberty interest such as the interest in privacy or the interest in freedom from restraint. *See Paul v. Davis*, 424 U.S. 693 (1976).

Answer (A) is not an accurate statement because the strength or legitimacy of any governmental or public interest is relevant to what procedures may be necessary; but is not central to the question whether a person's due process rights are triggered. *See Matthews v. Eldridge*, 424 U.S. 319 (1976).

Answer (B) is not an accurate statement. Disputed facts are essential to a right to a due process hearing. However, the question explains that placement in the registry is intended to warn the public that the individual is a "dangerous person." Convicted sex offenders thus have a strong argument that a disputed fact exists as to whether they "currently" are dangerous.

Answer (C) is not an accurate statement. Agency action creating a "stigma" (meaning damage to a person's reputation relating to immorality, dishonesty, criminality, etc.) does not itself trigger due process rights. *See Paul v. Davis*, 424 U.S. 693 (1976).

3.20. **Answer (D) is the most accurate description** of the *Matthews* test. The Court in *Matthews v. Eldridge*, 424 U.S. 319 (1976), stated that three factors should be considered: (i) the private interest, (ii) the risk of erroneous deprivation currently faced given procedural protections and the value of additional protections or safeguards, and (iii) the public interest, including fiscal and administrative burdens that would result from additional protections or safeguards.

Answer (A) is partially correct, but it is not the most accurate statement because it omits the factor of risk of error.

Answer (B) is not an accurate statement. These two factors are not balanced against one another; but, rather, these factors together help reflect the strength or importance of the private interests at stake.

Answer (C) is not an accurate statement. Similar to Answer (B), these two factors are not balanced against one another; but, rather, these factors together help reflect the strength or importance of the private interests at stake.

Judicial Review of Agency Adjudications

3.21. **Answer (D) is the best answer** because Answers (A), (B), and (C) are all accurate statements.

Answer (A) is an accurate statement. The facts state that the agency must follow formal APA procedures. Section 706(2)(E)'s substantial evidence standard applies in cases subject to formal APA procedures.

Answer (B) is an accurate statement. A court may always set aside agency action that is arbitrary and capricious. *See Citizens to Preserve Overton Park v. Volpe*, 401 U.S. 420 (1971).

Answer (C) is an accurate statement. A finding of "full and adequate" disclosure in this case is a "mixed" question of the sort discussed by the Supreme Court in *NLRB v. Hearst*, 322 U.S. 111 (1944). Thus, even if the underlying pure factual findings necessary to the determination are supported by sufficient evidence in the record, the court may assess the determination for reasonableness in light of legal principles relevant to when a disclosure is adequate.

3.22. **Answer (A) is an accurate statement.** Prior to the enactment of the APA, the Supreme Court interpreted the substantial evidence standard as requiring only consideration of the evidence supporting the agency decision. *See Consolidated Edison Co. v. NLRB*, 305 U.S. 197 (1938). However, § 706 provides that a reviewing court shall review "the whole record or those parts of it cited by a party. . . ." Thus, in *Universal Camera Corp. v. NLRB*, 340 U.S. 474 (1951), the Court explained that Congress intended to allow courts to set aside agency action if the evidence supporting the agency decision is not substantial when viewed in light of the evidence contrary to the agency's position.

Answer (B) is not an accurate statement for the reason noted above.

Answer (C) is not an accurate statement. The substantial evidence standard is a deferential standard of review. However, the standard is similar to that used by a court when deciding whether to grant a directed verdict in a civil action. In applying that standard, a court is not "weighing" the evidence.

Answer (D) is incorrect, because Answer (A) is an accurate statement.

3.23. **Answer (B) represents a more sound judicial response** for the reasons noted below.

Answer (A) is not the most sound judicial response. In applying the substantial evidence standard, a difficulty arises when the decision maker on the agency appeal and the ALJ disagree on a finding of fact. A court must proceed carefully when the agency reaches a conclusion opposite from that reached by the "impartial experienced examiner who has observed the witnesses and lived with the case." However, courts have rejected an absolute rule that the finding must be set aside if it rests on testimonial evidence discredited by the ALJ, even if the ALJ's credibility inferences were based on witness demeanor. *See, e.g., Universal Camera Corp. v. NLRB*, 340 U.S. 474 (1951) (noting, "[w]e intend only to recognize that evidence supporting a conclusion may be less substantial" when the agency finding is contrary to the ALJ's credibility determination").

Answer (C) does not reflect a sound judicial response because the agency is not bound by the ALJ's findings, even those grounded in credibility determinations.

Answer (D) does not reflect a sound judicial response. The ALJ's findings become a part of the record. Section 557(c) provides that "all decisions, including initial, recommended, or tentative decisions, are a part of the record . . .;" and, requires a statement of "findings and conclusions, and the reasons or basis therefor, on all the material issues of fact, law, or discretion presented. . . ."

3.24.   **Answer (D) is best answer,** because Answers (B) and (C) are accurate statements.

Answer (A) is not an accurate statement. Section 706(2)(E)'s substantial evidence standard applies in cases subject to formal APA procedures. In cases of informal adjudication, § 706(2)(A) applies, allowing a court to set aside agency findings and conclusions found to be arbitrary and capricious.

Answer (B) is an accurate statement. A court may always set aside agency action that is arbitrary and capricious. *See Citizens to Preserve Overton Park v. Volpe,* 401 U.S. 420 (1971).

Answer (C) is an accurate statement. A finding of "full and adequate" disclosure in this case is a "mixed" question of the sort discussed by the Supreme Court in *NLRB v. Hearst,* 322 U.S. 111 (1944). Thus, even if the underlying pure factual findings necessary to the determination are supported by sufficient evidence in the record, the court may assess the determination for reasonableness in light of legal principles relevant to when a disclosure is adequate.

3.25.   **Answer (B) is an accurate statement.** In *Overton Park,* the Court recognized that, in cases of informal adjudication, whatever record existed at the time the agency decision was made might not disclose the factors considered by the agency; and, thus, that it might be necessary for a court to require some explanation to aid in judicial review of the agency action. Further, the Court did not close the door on mandating testimony in a case where no contemporaneous explanation was made. However, the Court also suggested that other less objectionable means likely would suffice — such as allowing the agency to prepare post hoc "formal findings," as long as the reviewing court viewed them critically. *See Citizens to Preserve Overton Park v. Volpe,* 401 U.S. 420 (1971).

Answer (C) is an accurate statement. In light of the Court's sentiment expressed in *Overton Park,* regarding the need for an explanation of the basis for an agency's decision in order to properly provide judicial review — and the possibility of being required to submit to examination if necessary — agencies are likely to prepare a contemporaneous explanation of the basis for their findings and conclusions, even in cases involving informal adjudications. *See Citizens to Preserve Overton Park v. Volpe,* 401 U.S. 420 (1971).

Answer (A) is not an accurate statement. The Supreme Court in *Overton Park* clarified that this form of post hoc rationalization would be an inadequate basis for judicial review. *See Citizens to Preserve Overton Park v. Volpe,* 401 U.S. 420 (1971). Section 706 requires courts conducting judicial review to review the whole record — even in cases involving informal adjudication. Litigation affidavits are not part of the record.

Answer (D) is not an accurate statement for the reasons noted above.

3.26.   Yes. Section 705 of the APA specifically empowers courts to "issue all necessary and appropriate process to postpone the effective date of an agency action or to preserve status or rights" during the pendency of the judicial review — "on such conditions as may be required and to the extent necessary to prevent irreparable injury." *See* APA § 705.

3.27   **Answer (C) is an accurate statement.** The Court in *Gonzales* stated that *Chevron* deference is "warranted only 'when it appears that Congress delegated authority to the agency generally to make rules carrying the force of law, and that the agency interpretation claiming deference was promulgated in the exercise of that authority.'" *See* 546 U.S. 243 (2006). Because Customs has pointed to generally conferred authority to promulgate substantive regulations, the requisite congressional delegation exists. However, formulation of an interpretation in a civil enforcement action likely would not be considered an exercise of the authority to make rules with the force of law. The Court in *Mead* noted that *Chevron* deference has most often been applied to "the fruits of notice-and-comment rulemaking or formal adjudication." *See* 533 U.S. 218 (2001). Although the Court also stated that the lack of such procedures was not dispositive, the *Mead* Court's application of the standard suggests that formulation of the agency's interpretation of the Tariff Act in a routine in rem forfeiture action in a local federal district court would be insufficient to trigger *Chevron* deference. However, some level of deference may be appropriate, and the *Skidmore* factors help a court to decide that issue. *See United States v. Able Time, Inc.*, 545 F3d 824 (9th Cir. 2008) (from which the facts of this question were drawn). *See also Doe v. Leavitt*, 552 F.3d 75 (1st Cir. 2009) (for a case discussing and applying the Skidmore factors).

Answer (A) is not an accurate statement. The Court has clarified that *Chevron* deference is limited to an interpretation of a statute made by an agency under circumstances that would warrant *Chevron's* more generous deference. Thus, additional circumstances must be articulated.

Answer (B) is not an accurate statement. Although an agency interpretation may carry the force of law — and if so, it would be binding on a court — whether this particular agency interpretation in fact has the force of law is an issue to be decided in this judicial action. For the reason explained above, formulation in the course of this particular enforcement action likely would not satisfy the standard set forth in *Gonzales*.

Answer (D) is not an accurate statement. The Supreme Court has stated that agency interpretations articulated in the course of agency adjudications and enforcement actions may be entitled to some level of judicial deference. *See, e.g., Auer v. Robbins*, 519 U.S. 452 (1997).

4.1.   **Answer (A) is correct** because it represents the classical statement of retroactivity.

   Answer (B) is incorrect. It involves a classical statement of prospectivity; a new rule is announced, but is applied only to future activities.

   Answer (C) is incorrect. This is another example of prospectivity, provided that the case does not involve facts that arose prior to passage of the law.

   Answer (D) is incorrect because it states that "all of the above" involve retroactive laws, and, as noted, Answer (A) is the only one.

4.2.   **Answer (D) is the best answer.**

   Answers (A), (B), and (C) are not the best answers. While correct in that Answers (A), (B), and (C) identify some of the vices of retroactive laws — they deprive regulated entities of advance "notice" regarding the content and meaning of laws; they deprive regulated entities of a fair opportunity to bring their conduct into compliance with the law; and they are, therefore, less likely to be consistent with fair process — Answer (D) is the only answer to refer to all of these vices. *See* Russell L. Weaver, *Retroactive Regulatory Interpretations: An Analysis of Judicial Responses*, 61 Notre Dame L. Rev. 167 (1986).

4.3.   **Answer (D) is correct.** The due process clauses of the Fifth and Fourteenth amendments to the United States Constitution both prohibit retroactivity. While the prohibition is not explicit, it reflects the fact that citizens are entitled to fair notice of laws limiting their conduct, as well as to an opportunity to conform their conduct to those laws. When a law is applied retroactively, without providing notice and an opportunity to comply, there is a lack of "due process." *See* Russell L. Weaver, *Retroactive Regulatory Interpretations: An Analysis of Judicial Responses*, 61 *Notre Dame L. Rev.* 167 (1986).

   Answers (A) and (C) are essentially throw-away answers because there is nothing in either of those two clauses which explicitly or implicitly prohibits retroactivity.

   Answer (B) is incorrect, but some analysis is necessary. On its face, the First Amendment protects various rights including freedom of speech, freedom of religion, and the right to peacefully assemble. On their face, these rights provide no protection against retroactive application. However, because the courts treat these rights as "fundamental" and necessary to a free society, courts are very protective of these rights. As a result, courts give special emphasis to the due process prohibition against retroactivity as applied to those rights. But, on its own, the

First Amendment does not prohibit retroactivity.

4.4.   **Answer (C) is correct.** In fact, despite the vices of retroactive laws, retroactivity is not always impermissible. Courts balance the vices of retroactivity against the benefits and sometimes conclude that retroactivity is permissible.

   Answers (A) and (B) are incorrect because they suggest that retroactivity is either "always" or "never" constitutional, and the correct answer is "sometimes."

   Answer (D) is incorrect because it suggests that "none of the above" answers are correct, and Answer (C) is correct. *See National Labor Relations Board v. Bell Aerospace Company Division of Textron Inc.*, 416 U.S. 267 (1974).

4.5.   The norm for judicial decisions is retroactivity. Nevertheless, there has been much litigation about whether, and when, administrative agencies are allowed to apply their decisions prospectively. *See NLRB v. Wyman-Gordon Co.*, 394 U.S. 759 (1969). As a result, administrative decisions are usually applied retroactively unless to do so would deprive a regulated entity of adequate notice (and an opportunity to comply) or perpetuate unfairness. *See* Russell L. Weaver, *Retroactive Regulatory Interpretations: An Analysis of Judicial Responses*, 61 *Notre Dame L. Rev.* 167 (1986). Neither would occur here because the rule refers to "inhumane conditions" and shipping puppies at temperatures in excess of 90 degrees without air conditioning might be regarded as "inhumane."

4.6.   For legislative-type enactments, including administrative rules, the norm is prospective application. While it is possible to apply administrative rules retroactively, such application is rare and generally disfavored. This is especially true in the present case because the interpretation is implicit in the regulatory scheme.

4.7.   **Answer (C) is correct.** The practice regarding informal policies and interpretations is variable. It is not uncommon for administrative agencies to try to apply such policies and interpretations retroactively, but courts do not always permit retroactive application. *See* Because Answer (C) is correct (interpretations are "sometimes applied retroactively), it necessarily follows that **Answers (A), (B) and (D)**, which state that such interpretations are "never," "always," or "frequently" applied retroactively, **are incorrect**.

4.8.   **Answer (B) is correct.** *Bell Aerospace* held that the due process clause of the United States Constitution does not necessarily prohibit administrative agencies from applying adjudicative rules retroactively. However, in assessing whether retroactive application is permissible, a reviewing court must weigh the benefits of retroactive application (which can involve the need for retroactivity in the regulatory scheme) against the "mischief" that it would cause. *See National Labor Relations Board v. Bell Aerospace Company Division of Textron Inc.*, 416 U.S. 267 (1974).

   Answer (A) is incorrect because, while the agency's choice of whether to apply an adjudicative rule retroactively is a factor to be considered, it is not necessarily determinative. Even if an agency prefers to apply an adjudicative rule retroactively, a reviewing court might refuse to allow it to do so when the retroactive application would create undue mischief.

Answer (C) is incorrect because, while the fact that a regulated entity will suffer harm is a factor to be considered, it is not determinative of whether an adjudicative rule can be applied retroactively. Even if there is injury, a court might still permit retroactive application.

Answer (D) is incorrect. Because Answer (B) is correct, Answer (D), which states that "none of the above" is correct, is necessarily incorrect.

4.9. **Answer (A) is correct.** The United States Supreme Court has applied *Bell Aerospace's* benefit-mischief test not only to adjudicative rules, but also to legislative rules and informal agency rules and policies. *See National Labor Relations Board v. Bell Aerospace Company Division of Textron Inc.*, 416 U.S. 267 (1974).

Answer (B) is incorrect because it indicates that the analysis applies only to adjudicative rules, and it is in fact applied as well to "legislative rules and informal agency policies and interpretations."

Answer (C) is incorrect because it indicates that the analysis does not apply to "informal agency policies and interpretations."

Answer (D) is incorrect because it indicates that the analysis does not apply to legislative rules.

4.10. **Answer (D) is correct.** *Retail, Wholesale and Department Store Union v. National Labor Relations Board*, 466 F. 2d 380 (D.C. Cir. 1972), identified all of these factors (and two more) as relevant to the benefit-mischief analysis.

Answers (A), (B), and (C) are not the best answers. While correct in that they identify factors to be considered in the analysis, they do not go far enough because all three identify relevant factors, and only Answer (D) references each of them.

4.11. Under both *National Labor Relations Board v. Bell Aerospace Company Division of Textron Inc.*, 416 U.S. 267 (1974), and *Retail, Wholesale and Department Store Union v. National Labor Relations Board*, 466 F. 2d 380 (D.C. Cir. 1972), the courts are likely to find that the benefits of applying the rule retroactively outweigh the mischief. Especially important to the analysis are the facts that the agency has consistently inter preted the rule consistently with its present position and that it has published these prior applications. In other words, the regulated entity should have been aware of the agency's position and cannot claim surprise.

4.12. The answer to this question is debatable. Unquestionably, the regulation suffers from vagueness because it is difficult to know what the terms "excessively high temperature" and "humane" conditions mean. A reasonable person might have interpreted those terms to prohibit shipments only when the temperature was quite high (95 degrees to 100 degrees), but might also have interpreted the regulation as the DOA interpreted it (to prohibit shipments in 90 degree heat). Had

Wild West sought an official interpretive ruling from the agency, and had the agency issued the interpretation indicating that Wild West was free to ship the puppies under these conditions, the new interpretation would have represented an abrupt departure from the agency's prior interpretations and retroactivity would have been impermissible. The difficulty in this case is that Wild West did not seek a formal interpretive ruling, but instead made inquiry of a low-level employee, and so there is doubt about whether Wild West can or should rely on such advice. Regardless, Wild West is likely to prevail on its retroactivity claim because the process for seeking formal interpretive rulings is slow, laborious, and time consuming, and it was highly unlikely that Wild West could have obtained an interpretive ruling from DOA in time. Having done the best it could in terms of seeking advice (e.g., relying on the advice of a low-level employee), Wild West should not be subject to the retroactive application of the agency's newly stated position.

4.13.   **Answer (D) is the best answer.** Since Answers (A) and (B) are correct, and Answer (D) is the only answer to reference them both, Answer (D) is necessarily the correct answer.

Answers (A) and (B) are correct but are not the best answer. As the court stated in *Retail, Wholesale and Department Store Union v. National Labor Relations Board*, 466 F. 2d 380 (D.C. Cir. 1972), the two factors suggested in Answers (A) and (B) are highly relevant to the retroactivity analysis. The fact that an interpretation is implicit in a regulatory scheme, even though it has never been explicitly articulated, bears on whether the interpretation took the defendant by surprise. Likewise, the fact that the interpretation represents a radical departure from the SEC's prior interpretations of the securities laws is highly relevant.

Answer (C) is incorrect because the fact that the SEC likes or dislikes the regulated entity is completely irrelevant.

4.14.   In *Retail, Wholesale and Department Store Union v. National Labor Relations Board*, 466 F. 2d 380 (D.C. Cir. 1972), the Court held that the NLRB should not be allowed to apply the decision in *NLRB v. Fleetwood Trailer Co.*, 389 U.S. 375 (1967) retroactively.

The Court stated that:

> The standard to which the Company attempted to conform its conduct in this case was well established and long accepted by the Board. Unlike *Chenery*, this is not the kind of case where the Board "had not previously been confronted by the problem" and was required by the very absence of a previous standard and the nature of its duties to exercise the "function of filling in the interstices of the Act." Rather it is a case where the Board had confronted the problem before, had established an explicit standard of conduct, and now attempts to punish conformity to that standard under a new standard subsequently adopted.

5.1.   **Answer (D) is the best answer.** Answers (A), (B), and (C) are technically correct and therefore Answer (D) is the best answer.

Answer (C) is correct. The Administrative Procedure Act does not define the term "non-legislative rule." Defined literally, a non-legislative rule is one that is not promulgated "legislatively."

Answers (A) and (B) are also correct because some examples of non-legislative rules are adjudicative rules and agency policy statements and interpretations.

5.2.   **Answer (A) is correct.** Although courts frequently urge administrative agencies to avoid creating new rules by non-legislative means, and encourage them to create those rules legislatively, the non-legislative mechanism is an extremely effective mechanism for announcing policy. *See, e.g., Chenery II: A Forty-Year Retrospective*, 40 Ad. L. Rev. 161 (1988). As a result, most administrative agencies use that mechanism frequently.

Answers (B), (C), and (D) are incorrect because they state that non-legislative rules are created "never," "sometimes," or "always."

5.3.   **Answer (D) is the best answer.**

Answers (A), (B), and (C) are correct but are not the best answer. In *Chenery II*, the Court articulated each of the propositions stated in Answers (A), (B), and (C). Because agencies cannot articulate all policy legislatively, but still need to fill-in the interstices of their regulatory schemes, agencies have discretion about whether to articulate new rules legislatively or non-legislatively. *See SEC v. Chenery Corp.*, 332 U.S. 194 (1947) (*Chenery II*). Therefore, Answer (D), "all of the above," is necessarily correct. *See, e.g., Chenery II: A Forty-Year Retrospective*, 40 Ad. L. Rev. 161 (1988).

5.4.   **Answer (B) is correct.** *Chenery II* held that administrative agencies may create new rules either legislatively or adjudicatively (adjudication is a form of non-legislative rule-making), and that the choice between those procedures is a matter of agency discretion. *See SEC v. Chenery Corp.*, 332 U.S. 194 (1947) (*Chenery II*). *Chenery II* was reinforced by the Court's later holding in *National Labor Relations Board v. Bell Aerospace Company Division of Textron Inc.*, 416 U.S. 267 (1974).

Answer (A) is incorrect because it suggests that administrative agencies must use legislative procedures whenever possible.

Answer (C) is incorrect because it indicates that non-legislative procedures may be used only as a last resort.

Answer (D), "all of the above," is necessarily incorrect since Answers (A) and (C) are incorrect.

5.5. **Answer (D) is the best answer.** In *Chenery II*, the Court articulated all of these ideas. *See SEC v. Chenery Corp.*, 332 U.S. 194 (1947) *(Chenery II)*. Review the subparts to this question because they provide much insight into the reasons why courts permit agencies to promulgate rules legislatively.

Answers (A), (B), and (C) are all correct insofar as they go, but only Answer (D) identifies all of the relevant factors.

5.6. **Answer (D) is the best answer.** Again, *Chenery II* articulated all of these propositions. *See SEC v. Chenery Corp.*, 332 U.S. 194 (1947) *(Chenery II)*.

Answers (A), (B), and (C) are correct, but none identifies all of these propositions except Answer (D).

5.7. In *Chenery II*, the Court urged agencies to proceed as much as possible by legislative rule, but many agencies prefer to articulate policy by non-legislative means. *See SEC v. Chenery Corp.*, 332 U.S. 194 (1947) *(Chenery II)*. There are a number of reasons. One of the reasons that agencies prefer to use the non-legislative process is that it allows them to produce "rules" much more quickly. Although the informal (notice and com ment) rulemaking process can be quick, it can get complicated if powerful interests (e.g., large corporations) are affected by the proposed rule. These powerful interests can submit detailed reports and comments and make the process much more complex. Although some commentators argue that the legislative process produces clearer and more precise rules, there is no inherent reason why the legislative process should produce clearer or more precise rules. In a given case, an agency's non-legislative rule may be clearer and more precise than its legislative rule. *Id.*

5.8. **Answer (C) is correct.** It states that adjudicative procedures cannot be used to create bright line rules, and it is possible to use adjudicative procedures to create such rules. This is an invalid criticism. There is no reason why an agency cannot create bright line rules using adjudicative procedures. While agencies may be less likely to create bright line rules using adjudicative procedures, because the adjudicative process is designed to produce a decision on particular facts, there is no inherent reason why the agency cannot do so. *See, e.g., Chenery II: A Forty-Year Retrospective*, 40 Ad. L. Rev. 161 (1988).

Answer (A) is incorrect because it is a valid criticism. Adjudicative procedures frequently produce rules that are applied retroactively. *See* Russell L. Weaver, *Retroactive Regulatory Interpretations: An Analysis of Judicial Responses*, 61 Notre Dame L. Rev. 167 (1986).

Answer (B) is incorrect because it is also a valid criticism. Adjudicative procedures often single out one regulated entity for regulatory action. *See, e.g., Chenery II: A Forty-Year Retrospective*, 40 Ad. L. Rev. 161 (1988).

Answer (D) is incorrect because it states that "none of the above" is correct and Answer (C) is correct.

5.9. **Answer (D) is correct.**

Answers (A), (B), and (C) are incorrect because they all state reasons why an agency might be motivated to avoid legislative processes. *See, e.g., Chenery II: A Forty-Year Retrospective*, 40 Ad. L. Rev. 161 (1988). As a result, **Answer (D), "none of the above," is the only correct answer.**

5.10. It is simply not correct to state that courts treat non-legislative rules as binding or that they never treat them as binding. As will be discussed more fully below, courts some times give deference to non-legislative rules so that regulated entities cannot treat them lightly or disregard them. *See* Russell L. Weaver, *Some Realism About Chevron*, 58 Mo. L. Rev. 130 (1993).

5.11. **Answer (D) is the best answer** because Answers (A), (B), and (C) are all correct.

Answer (A) is correct because courts treat non-legislative rules differently depending on the format in which they are stated. *See* Russell L. Weaver, *Chevron, Martin, Anthony and Format Requirements*, 40 Kan. L. Rev. 587 (1992); Russell L. Weaver, *Evaluating Regulatory Interpretations: Individual Statements*, 80 Ky. L.J. 987 (1991–92).

Answer (B) is correct (although some may disagree) because deference principles are so inconsistently applied. *See* Russell L. Weaver, *Some Realism About Chevron*, 58 Mo. L. Rev. 130 (1993).

Answer (C) is correct because the status of the issuing official can affect how the courts treat an interpretive statement. *See* Russell L. Weaver, *Evaluating Regulatory Interpretations: Individual Statements*, 80 Ky. L.J. 987 (1991–92).

5.12. In general, courts allow agencies to change the content of their non-legislative rules, and allow them to do so by non-legislative means. In other words, they do not require agen cies to use legislative procedures (e.g., notice and comment procedures) to alter or change their non-legislative rules. *See* Russell L. Weaver, *A Foolish Consistency is the Hobgoblin of Little Minds*, 44 Baylor L. Rev. 529 (1992).

5.13. **Answer (A) is correct.** *NLRB v. Wyman-Gordon Co.*, 394 U.S. 759 (1969) is a strange decision in many important respects. Although the Court castigated the NLRB for the procedures used, it ultimately upheld the agency's action because it applied the announced rule in the case before it. *See* Russell L. Weaver, *Chenery II: A Forty-Year Retrospective*, 40 Ad. L. Rev. 161 (1988). The Court did suggest that it might have struck the rule down had it been applied purely prospectively. *See NLRB v. Wyman-Gordon Co.*, 394 U.S. 759 (1969).

Answer (B) is incorrect. Although the Court castigated the agency for using hybrid procedures, the Court did not hold that the NLRB was absolutely precluded from using such procedures provided, of course, that it applied the resulting rule in the case before it.

Answer (C) is incorrect. *Wyman-Gordon* did not hold that agencies may never articulate "rules" in adjudicative proceedings. *See NLRB v. Wyman-Gordon Co.*, 394 U.S. 759 (1969). Indeed, in order to render such a ruling, the Court would have been required to overrule its prior holding in *SEC v. Chenery Corp.*, 332 U.S. 194 (1947). The Court did not go that far. *See, e.g., Chenery II: A Forty-Year Retrospective*, 40 Ad. L. Rev. 161 (1988).

Answer (D) is incorrect because it states that "none of the above" is correct, and Answer (A) is correct.

5.14.   **Answer (B) is correct** because agencies frequently use non-legislative procedures to articulate new rules and policies.

Answer (A) is incorrect because, as *Chenery II* held, agencies have discretion to articulate policy by non-legislative means. *See SEC v. Chenery Corp.*, 332 U.S. 194 (1947). So, the concept of a non-legislative rule is not an oxymoron.

Answer (C) is incorrect because agencies frequently use non-legislative procedures even in non-emergency situations. *Id.*

Answer (D) is necessarily incorrect because some of the prior answers are incorrect.

5.15.   **Answer (D) is correct.** None of the statements in Answers (A), (B), and (C) are correct, and therefore Answer (D), "none of the above," is the correct answer.

Answer (A) is incorrect because neither the APA, nor judicially imposed rules, require agencies to allow the public to have input regarding the content of non-legislative rules. *See, e.g., Chenery II: A Forty-Year Retrospective*, 40 Ad. L. Rev. 161 (1988).

Answer (B) is incorrect as well, although some might debate the issue. A number of commentators would argue that non-legislative rules cannot create binding requirements. *Id.* Indeed, some courts hold that non-legislative rules that attempt to create binding rules are nothing more than disguised legislative rules. *Id.* And, because these disguised legislative rules have not been created by rulemaking procedures, they are invalid. The reality is that agencies often articulate policy by non-legislative means, sometimes treat those rules as binding, and are sometimes upheld by the courts. *See, generally*, Russell L. Weaver, *Some Realism about Chevron*, 58 Mo. L. Rev. 130 (1993).

Answer (C) is incorrect. At certain times, regulated entities ignore non-legislative rules at their peril. *Id.*

5.16.   **Answer (A) is correct** because non-legislative rules (by definition) are not subject to notice and comment procedures which are legislative procedures. *See, e.g., Chenery II: A Forty-Year Retrospective*, 40 Ad. L. Rev. 161 (1988).

Answers (B) and (C) are incorrect because the APA does mandate application of those procedure to non-legislative rules. *Id.*

Answer (D) is incorrect because it states "all of the above."

5.17. **Answer (D) is the best answer.**

Answers (A), (B), and (C) are all correct. All of these ideas were explicitly articulated in the *Chevron* case. *See Chevron v. Natural Resources Defense Council, Inc.*, 467 U.S. 837 (1984). Therefore, only Answer (D), "none of the above," is correct.

5.18. **Answer (B) is correct.** *Chevron* was explicit on this point. *See Chevron v. Natural Resources Defense Council, Inc.*, 467 U.S. 837 (1984).

Answers (A) and (C) are incorrect because they articulate different and lower standards of deference and thus they are necessarily inconsistent with *Chevron v. Natural Resources Defense Council, Inc.*, 467 U.S. 837 (1984).

Answer (D) is incorrect. Because some of the answers are incorrect, Answer (D), which states "all of the above," is necessarily incorrect.

5.19. **Answer (A) is correct.** *Skidmore* contained the very language set forth in Answer (A), and therefore that answer is correct. *See Skidmore v. Swift & Co.*, 323 U.S. 134 (1944).

Answers (B) and (C) are incorrect because they articulate standards of review that are different than that set forth in Answer (A).

Answer (D) is incorrect because it indicates that "none of the above" is correct, and Answer (A) is correct.

5.20. **Answer (C) is correct.** *Skidmore* held that the courts should consider the mixture of factors set forth in Answer (C), and therefore that answer is necessarily correct. *Skidmore v. Swift & Co.*, 323 U.S. 134 (1944).

Answer (A) is not the best answer though it is arguably correct because congressional intent is an important factor to be considered. However, *Skidmore* did not hold that it was the primary factor. *Id.* Instead, the Court indicated that the focus should be only the factors set forth in Answer (C). *Id.*

Answer (B) is incorrect because the importance attached by the agency is not the primary factor.

Answer (D) is incorrect is necessarily incorrect because Answer (C) is correct.

5.21. **Answer (B) is correct.** Format issues can be determinative, so Answer (B) is correct. *See* Russell L. Weaver, *Chevron, Martin, Anthony and Format Requirements*, 40 Kan. L. Rev. 587 (1992).

Answer (A) is incorrect because the agency's wishes are not the controlling factor.

Answer (C) is incorrect because the United States Supreme Court does not focus primarily on the wishes of the reviewing judge.

Answer (D) is incorrect. Answer (D), which indicates that "none of the above," is correct, is necessarily incorrect since Answer (B) is correct.

5.22. **Answer (B) is correct.** *Christensen v. Harris County*, 529 U.S. 576 (2000) deferred to an interpretation set forth in an opinion letter.

Answers (A), (C), and (D) are incorrect because the case did not involve deference to an interpretation stated in those formats.

5.23. **Answer (B) is correct.** The answer to this question is debatable. However, a number of courts have held that a non-legislative rule becomes a legislative rule (and usually an invalid one if legislative procedures have not been complied with) when an agency purports to create a binding duty. *See* W. FUNK, S. SHAPIRO & R. WEAVER, ADMINISTRATIVE PRACTICE AND PROCEDURE: PROBLEMS AND CASES 342–45 (West, 2d ed. 1997).

Answers (A) and (C) are incorrect because courts do not hold that such actions create legislative rules. *Id.*

Answer (D) is incorrect. Because Answer (B) is correct, Answer (D) which states "none of the above" is necessarily incorrect.

5.24. Given that a non-legislative rule can reflect the considered view of the agency responsible for a regulatory scheme, and given that courts frequently accept such rules, it is reasonable for regulated entities to rely on them. Indeed, if the regulated entity relies, and the agency subsequently shifts its position, courts may prevent the agency from applying the rule retroactively. *See* Russell L. Weaver, *Retroactive Regulatory Interpretations: An Analysis of Judicial Responses*, 61 Notre Dame L. Rev. 167 (1986).

5.25. There is no clear-cut response that courts always take. Sometimes, courts will hold that an agency has discretion to alter its interpretation. At other times, the courts will preclude retroactive application on the basis of the unfairness. The most likely response is the latter: the court will preclude retroactive application of the new interpretation. *See* Russell L. Weaver, *Retroactive Regulatory Interpretations: An Analysis of Judicial Responses*, 61 *Notre Dame L. Rev.* 167 (1986).

5.26. **Answer (C) is correct.** In *Bowles*, the Court was explicit on this point. *See Bowles v. Seminole Sand & Rock Co.*, 325 U.S. 410 (1945).

Answer (A) is incorrect because *Bowles* did not hold that agencies could exercise unfettered discretion. *Id.*

Answer (B) is incorrect because *Bowles* did not involve a question of statutory interpretation. *Id.*

Answer (D) is incorrect because *Bowles* did not hold that agency interpretations were entitled to no deference in this context. *Id.*

5.27. **Answer (D) is the best answer.** Courts have deferred to interpretations stated in all of these formats. *See* Russell L. Weaver, *Chevron, Martin, Anthony and Format Requirements*, 40 Kan. L. Rev. 587 (1992).

Answers (A), (B), and (C) are correct, but Answer (D) is the best answer.

6.1.   **Answer (D) is the best answer.** All of these statements are aspects of jurisdiction. *See* W. FUNK, S. SHAPIRO & R. WEAVER, ADMINISTRATIVE PRACTICE AND PROCEDURE: PROBLEMS AND CASES 403–04 (West, 2d ed. 1997).

       Answers (A), (B), and (C) are all correct, but Answer (D) is the best answer since it encompassed all three correct answers.

6.2.   **Answer (B) is correct** because the Administrative Procedure Act's review provisions can be regarded as creating a general grant of jurisdiction to review administrative action. *See* W. FUNK, S. SHAPIRO & R. WEAVER, ADMINISTRATIVE PRACTICE AND PROCEDURE: PROBLEMS AND CASES 404 (West, 2d ed. 1997).

       Answer (A) is incorrect because the general federal jurisdictional statute is not regarded as establishing a cause of action against administrative agencies. *Id.*

       Answer (C) is incorrect because, in many instances, agency's governing statutes specifically contain jurisdictional provisions. *Id.*

       Answer (D) is incorrect. Because Answer (B) is correct, Answer (D), which states "none of the above" is correct, is necessarily incorrect.

6.3.   **Answer (A) is correct.** In fact, when an agency's governing statute contains a provision granting judicial review, that provision may also be construed as creating a cause of action. *See* W. FUNK, S. SHAPIRO & R. WEAVER, ADMINISTRATIVE PRACTICE AND PROCEDURE: PROBLEMS AND CASES 403–04 (West, 2d ed. 1997).

       Answer (B) is incorrect because courts do not have inherent authority to review administrative action, and there is no common law (non-statutory) right of review. *Id.*

       Answer (C) is incorrect because the APA can be used as the basis for creating a cause of action. *Id.*

       Answer (D) is incorrect. Because Answer (A) is correct, Answer (D), which suggests that "none of the above" is correct, is necessarily incorrect.

6.4.   **Answer (D) is the best answer.** All of these statements correctly summarize the requirements to establish review under the APA. *See* W. FUNK, S. SHAPIRO & R. WEAVER, ADMINISTRATIVE PRACTICE AND PROCEDURE: PROBLEMS AND CASES 404–05 (West, 2d ed. 1997).

       Answers (A), (B), and (C) are correct, as far as they go, but Answer (D) is a much preferable answer.

6.5.   **Answer (D) is the best answer.** In order to challenge administrative action, a plaintiff must show all of these things.

Answers (A), (B), and (C) are correct, as far as they go, but Answer (D) is a much preferable answer.

6.6.   **Answer (C) is correct.** To the extent that the standing doctrine is constitutionally based, rather than prudentially based, it is premised upon Article III's case and controversy requirement. *See United States v. Richardson*, 418 U.S. 166 (1974); *Sierra Club v. Morton*, 405 U.S. 727 (1972). As a result, it is not premised upon either the commerce clause (Answer (A)) or the due process clause (Answer (B)). *Id.* Answer (D), which refers to "all of the above," is therefore necessarily incorrect.

6.7.   **Answer (A) is correct.** In a number of cases, the Court has made it clear that standing requires prove that plaintiff is suffering injury and that a favorable judicial decision will redress that injury. *See Simon v. Eastern Kentucky Welfare Rights Organization*, 426 U.S. 26 (1976).

Answer (B) is incorrect. Although the Court applied the "legal wrong" theory at one point, it does no longer. *See Alexander Sprunt & Son v. United States*, 281 U.S. 249 (1930).

Answer (C) is incorrect. Ideological injury, by itself, provides an insufficient basis for challenging administrative action. *See United States v. Richardson*, 418 U.S. 166 (1974); *Sierra Club v. Morton*, 405 U.S. 727 (1972).

Answer (D) is incorrect because it refers to "all of the above" as being correct.

6.8.   **Answer (C) is correct.** *See Sierra Club v. Morton*, 405 U.S. 727 (1972).

Answer (A) is incorrect because it contradicts Answer (C). In *Sierra Club*, the Court concluded that injury to environmental, aesthetic, and recreational interests is sufficient injury. *Sierra Club v. Morton*, 405 U.S. 727 (1972).

Answer (B) is incorrect. As the Court also held in the *Sierra Club* ease, financial injury is not a prerequisite to standing. *Sierra Club v. Morton*, 405 U.S. 727 (1972).

Answer (D) is incorrect. Because Answer (C) is correct, Answer (D), which provides "none of the above" is correct, is necessarily incorrect.

6.9.   *Sierra Club* held that an association could represent the interests of its members, but only if it could show that one of them was suffering "injury in fact." As the previous question and answer demonstrate, the case also held that the required injury need not be financial, but could instead involve injury to environmental, aesthetic and recreational interests. *Sierra Club v. Morton*, 405 U.S. 727 (1972).

6.10.   In *Eastern Kentucky*, the Court denied relief because plaintiff could not show that, even if it obtained judicial relief, that the judicial award would redress the perceived injury. Absent such a showing the standing requirement is not satisfied. *See Simon v. Eastern Kentucky Welfare Rights Organization*, 426 U.S. 26 (1976).

6.11.   One person is not generally allowed to assert the rights of another. *See Tileston v.*

Ullman, 318 U.S. 44 (1943). However, there are limited situations when one person is allowed to assert and represent the rights of another. *See NAACP v. Alabama*, 357 U.S. 449 (1958). These usually involve situations where there is a relationship, in terms of rights or interest, between the parties so that the one is likely to be an effective advocate for the other (e.g., a doctor representing the interests of a plaintiff).

6.12.   **Answer (C) is correct.** Answer (C) and Answer (A) are directly contradictory. In the actual case, the Court held consistently with Answer (C): "Plaintiff cannot establish standing under the Endangered Species Act by showing that she once visited crocodiles in Egypt, intended to do so again, and believes that administrative action might irreparably affect her ability to do so." *Lujan v. Defenders of Wildlife*, 504 U.S. 555 (1992).

    Answer (A) is incorrect. *Lujan* concluded that, not only had plaintiffs failed to show imminent injury, they failed to show that a favorable judicial decision would redress that injury. *Lujan v. Defenders of Wildlife*, 504 U.S. 555 (1992).

    Answer (B) is incorrect. Since Answer (C), which states that plaintiff cannot establish standing, is correct, Answer (B) cannot be correct. It suggests that plaintiffs always have standing to challenge decisions under the Endangered Species Act.

    Answer (D) is incorrect. Of course, given that one of the answers is correct, Answer (D), which states that "none of the above" is correct, is necessarily incorrect.

6.13.   **Answer (B) is correct.** The Court held that the voters had standing because Congress intended to protect voters such as these, and that they were suffering injury in fact by their inability to obtain information. *Federal Election Commission v. Akins*, 524 U.S. 11 (1998). As a result, the Article III case and controversy requirement was satisfied. *Id.*

    Answer (A) is incorrect. Answer (A), which concludes that the voters do not have standing, is therefore necessarily inconsistent with the holding in the case. *Id.*

    Answer (C) is incorrect because the Court did not hold that the Article III "case and controversy" requirement is prudential rather than jurisdictional. *Id.*

    Answer (D) is incorrect. Because Answer (B) is correct, Answer (D), which states that "none of the above" is correct, is necessarily incorrect.

6.14.   **Answer (C) is the best answer.** Section 701(a) of the Administrative Procedure Act provides that judicial review is inapplicable when either Congress chooses to preclude review by statute or agency action is committed to agency discretion by law. 5 U.S.C. § 701(a).

    Answers (A) and (B) are technically correct. However, Answer (C) is more accurate since it sweeps in both Answer (A) and Answer (B).

    Answer (D) is incorrect. Answer (D), which suggests that neither Answer (A) nor Answer (B) is correct, is necessarily wrong.

6.15.   **Answer (C) is correct.** *Abbott Laboratories* held that the APA's judicial review provisions should be "hospitably interpreted to prohibit review only when there is "clear and convincing evidence" that Congress intended to restrict review. *Abbott Laboratories v. Gardner*, 387 U.S. 136 (1967).

Answers (A) and (B) are incorrect because Abbott did not state either of the propositions contained in those answers. *Id.*

Answer (D) is incorrect. Because Answer (C) is correct, Answer (D), which states that "none of the above" is correct, is necessarily wrong.

6.16.   In *Block v. Community Nutrition Institute*, 467 U.S. 340 (1984), the Court held that "dairy handlers" have standing to challenge the Secretary's milk market orders; consumers cannot challenge the Secretary's milk market orders; and dairy producers can challenge the Secretary's milk market orders. The Court concluded that Congress did not intend to prohibit review by either dairy handlers or dairy producers, but did intend to preclude review by consumers.

6.17.   **Answer (C) is correct.** Under the APA, interim judicial review is permissible only when the agency's governing statute provides for it. Otherwise, it is assumed that courts will only review final agency action. 5 U.S.C. § 704.

Answers (A) and (B) are incorrect because they provide that judicial review of interim action is either readily available or not available, and therefore neither Answer contains the nuances of the APA. *See* 5 U.S.C. § 704.

Answer (D) is incorrect. Because Answer (C) is correct, Answer (D), which states that "none of the above" is correct, is necessarily incorrect.

6.18.   In *Franklin v. Massachusetts*, 505 U.S. 788 (1992), the Court held that the Department's submission of census results to the President did not constitute final agency action because the statute did not require the President to use the data, as well as because the statute did not forbid the agency from further amending the data.

6.19.   In *McCarthy v. Madigan*, 503 U.S. 140 (1992), the Court held that exhaustion was not required since the interests of judicial economy will not be advanced given that the procedure does not create a formal factual record.

6.20.   In *Abbott Laboratories v. Gardner*, 387 U.S. 136 (1967), the Court held that the matter was ripe for review because the plaintiffs would be faced with the choice of incurring immediate compliance costs or facing the risk of criminal sanctions. The Court held that they should not be required to undergo this risk.

6.21.   In *Ohio Forestry Association, Inc. v. Sierra Club*, 523 U.S. 726 (1998), the Court held that the case was not ripe for review. The Court emphasized that NFMA had not completed its plan, and had not moved to implement it.

6.22.   In *Toilet Goods Association v. Gardner*, 387 U.S. 158 (1967), the Court held that the case was ripe for review. The Court concluded that pre-enforcement review was allowed because the manufacturers should not be forced to run the risk of being immediately suspended in order to challenge the regulation.

```
┌─────────────────────────────────────────────────────────────────────────┐
│  TOPIC 7:                                          ANSWERS                │
│                                                                           │
│  AGENCY STRUCTURE                                                         │
└─────────────────────────────────────────────────────────────────────────┘
```

7.1.   **Answer (C) is correct.** Although some might argue that administrative agencies constitute an independent fourth branch of government, the reality is that they are not independent. Moreover, there are only three branches of government. *See* W. Funk, S. Shapiro & R. Weaver, Administrative Practice and Procedure: Problems and Cases 506–67 (West, 2d ed. 1997).

      Answers (A) and (B) are incorrect because administrative agencies are usually located in the executive branch of government. *Id.*

      Answer (D) is incorrect. As we shall see in later questions, administrative agencies can be lodged in any of the three branches of government. *Id.*

7.2.   **Answer (B) is correct.** In *Panama Refining*, the Court was concerned about administrative agencies exercising unfettered and uncontrolled discretion, as well as about whether there was an "unlawful delegation" of power. *Panama Refining Co. v. Ryan*, 293 U.S. 388 (1935). As a result, the Court held that delegations of power must be accompanied by an "intelligible principle" in the form of a policy, standard or rule to guide the agency in the exercise of its discretion. *Id.* The Court found that there was no intelligible principle in the NIRA. *Id.*

      Answers (A) and (C) are incorrect because *Panama Refining* took a narrow view of Congress' power to delegate, and these answers contemplate a much broader and permissive perspective. *Id.*

      Answer (D) is incorrect. Because Answer (B) is correct, Answer (D), which states that "none of the above" is correct, is necessarily incorrect.

7.3.   **Answer (B) is correct.** *Schechter* reinforced the holding in *Panama Refining Co. v. Ryan*, 293 U.S. 388 (1935) and also reiterated the unlawful delegation doctrine. *A.L.A. Schechter Poultry Corp. v. United States*, 295 U.S. 495 (1935). In that case, the Court held that Congress may not delegate authority to the President to approve codes of fair competition without supplying an intelligible principle that limits the President's authority. *Id.* The Court found that there was no intelligible principle in the legislation in question. *Id.*

      Answer (A) is incorrect because it suggests that Congress has unquestioned authority to make the delegation. Obviously, Congress did not have unquestioned authority because the courts struck down the delegation. *Id.*

      Answer (C) is incorrect because it suggests, contrary to *Schechter*, that Congress may never delegate authority to the executive branch. *Id.*

      Answer (D) is incorrect. Because Answer (B) is correct, Answer (D), which states that "none of the above is correct, is necessarily incorrect.

7.4.   **Answer (B) is correct.** Both *Panama Refining Co. v. Ryan*, 293 U.S. 388 (1935), and *A.L.A. Schechter Poultry Corp. v. United States*, 295 U.S. 495 (1935), have been relegated to the dustbin of history. *See Mistretta v. United States*, 488 U.S. 361 (1989). In the 70 or so years since those cases were decided, the Court has been extremely reluctant to invoke the unlawful delegation doctrine. The Court stills talks about finding "intelligible principles," but it is much more willing to find those principles in later cases. *Id.*

Answers (A) and (C) are incorrect. Those delegations do not have continuing currency and vitality and are not about to stage a comeback. As Answer (B) correctly notes, they have been relegated to the dustbin of history. *See* W. FUNK, S. SHAPIRO & R. WEAVER, ADMINISTRATIVE PRACTICE AND PROCEDURE: PROBLEMS AND CASES 511–15 (West, 2d ed. 1997).

Answer (D) is incorrect. Because Answer (B) is correct, Answer (D), which suggests that "none of the above" is correct, is necessarily incorrect.

7.5.   **Answer (B) is correct.** All that the Court requires today is proof of some general principle.

Answer (A) is incorrect. Today, the Court is very unlikely to require precise delineation of the principle in the manner dictated by decisions like *Panama Refining Co. v. Ryan*, 293 U.S. 388 (1935), and *A.L.A. Schechter Poultry Corp. v. United States*, 295 U.S. 495 (1935). Those decisions have been relegated to the dustbin of history.

Answer (C) is incorrect. As a general rule, courts are quite capable of finding an "intelligible principle" in most delegations. *See Mistretta v. United States*, 488 U.S. 361 (1989).

Answer (D) is incorrect. Because Answer (B) is correct, Answer (D), which states that "none of the above" is correct, is necessarily incorrect.

7.6.   **Answer (C) is correct** because the courts have held that there judicial power is delegable provided that the delegation involves "public rights" rather than "private rights." *See Murray's Lessee v. Hoboken Land and Improvement Co.*, 59 U.S. (18 How.) 272 (1855).

Answer (A) is incorrect. The Court has held that administrative agencies can exercise judicial-type powers. *See Mistretta v. United States*, 488 U.S. 361 (1989).

Answer (B) is incorrect even though it was the law at one time. *Id.*

Answer (D) is incorrect. Because Answer (C) is correct, Answer (D), which states that "none of the above" is correct, is necessarily incorrect.

7.7.   **Answer (D) is the best answer.** In *Crowell v. Benson*, 285 U.S. 22 (1932), the Court held all of the propositions set forth in Answers (A), (B), and (C). As a result, Answer (D), which states that "all of the above" are correct, is the best answer.

7.8.   **Answer (C) is correct** because the Court has defined "public rights" as "rights which arise between the government and persons subject to its authority in connection with the performance of the constitutional functions of the executive or legislative departments." *See Crowell v. Benson*, 285 U.S. 22 (1932).

Answers (A) and (B) are incorrect because *Crowell* did not define "public rights" in that way. *See Crowell v. Benson*, 285 U.S. 22 (1932).

Answer (D) is incorrect. Because Answer (C) is correct, Answer (D), which states that "none of the above" is correct, is necessarily incorrect.

7.9.   **Answer (C) is correct.** The Court concluded that constitutional facts should be assigned to an Article III court. *Crowell v. Benson*, 285 U.S. 22 (1932).

Answer (A) is incorrect because the Court did not hold that, although the public rights/private rights distinction is important, courts should not slavishly adhere to it. *Id.*

Answer (B) is incorrect because the Court did not hold that "despite the public rights/private rights distinction, Congress should make every effort to assign judicial power solely to Article III courts." *Id.*

Answer (D) is incorrect. Because Answer (C) is correct, Answer (D), which states that "none of the above" is correct, is necessarily incorrect.

7.10.   **Answer (A) is correct.** The Court allowed the CFTC to hear this counterclaim. *Commodity Futures Trading Commission v. Schor*, 478 U.S. 833 (1986).

Answer (B) is incorrect because the Court did not hold that "the private rights/public rights distinction should always be treated as determinative in deciding whether adjudicative power could be delegated to a non-Article III body." *Id.*

Answer (C) is incorrect because the Court did not hold that a "delegation to the CFTC posed a substantial threat to the concept of separation of powers." *Id.*

Answer (D) is incorrect. Because Answer (A) is correct, Answer (D), which states that "none of the above" is correct, is necessarily incorrect.

7.11.   **Answer (B) is correct** because the Seventh Amendment protects the right to trial by jury. United States Constitution, Amendment Seven.

Answer (A) is incorrect because the Seventh Amendment does not state that "administrative agencies shall not impose cruel and unusual punishments." *See* United States Constitution, Amendment Seven.

Answer (C) is incorrect because the Seventh Amendment does not state that "administrative agencies shall not hold individuals on excessive bail." *See* United States Constitution, Amendment Seven.

Answer (D) is incorrect. Because Answer (B) is correct, Answer (D), which states that "none of the above" is correct, is necessarily incorrect.

7.12.   **Answer (B) is correct.** The Court did not require a jury trial in *Atlas Roofing*.

Atlas Roofing Co. v. Occupational Safety and Health Review Commission, 430 U.S. 442 (1977). As a result, the matter could be heard by an administrative agency even though agencies cannot grant jury trials. *Id.*

Answer (A) is incorrect because *Atlas Roofing* did not hold that the "Seventh Amendment mandates a jury trial before an administrative agency can impose a financial penalty under the Occupational Safety and Health Act." *Id.*

Answer (C) is incorrect because Atlas Roofing did not hold that "when Congress creates new statutory rights, it may not assign those rights to an administrative agency in which a jury trial would be incompatible." *Id.*

Answer (D) is incorrect. Because Answer (B) is correct, Answer (D), which states that "none of the above" is correct, is necessarily incorrect.

7.13.   **Answer (A) is correct** because, in *Atlas Roofing,* the Court held that, when Congress creates new statutory "public rights," it may assign the adjudication of those rights to an administrative agency with which a jury trial would be incompatible. *Atlas Roofing Co. v. Occupational Safety and Health Review Commission,* 430 U.S. 442 (1977).

Answer (B) is incorrect because *Atlas Roofing* did not hold that Congress can assign the adjudication of rights to an administrative body, to be heard without a jury, even though a jury would have been required had the case been heard by an Article III court. *Id.*

Answer (C) is incorrect because *Atlas Roofing* did not hold that "administrative adjudication of public rights do not constitute a suit at common law and is not in the nature of such a suit." *Id.*

Answer (D) is incorrect. Because Answers (B) and (C) are incorrect, Answer (D), which states that "all of the above" answers are correct, is necessarily incorrect.

7.14.   In *Immigration and Naturalization Service v. Chadha,* 462 U.S. 919 (1983), the Court held that the so-called "legislative veto," under which one house of Congress can veto administrative action is unconstitutional because it leaves the President out of the veto process. In order to overrule administrative action, Congress must pass legislation bicamerally (in other words, by both houses of Congress) and present it to the President for his signature.

7.15.   In *Myers v. United States,* 272 U.S. 52 (1926), the Court held that "the President's obligation to 'faithfully execute the laws' of the United States carries with it the power to remove 'officers' of the United States with the Senate's advice and consent." *Myers* rejected the proposition that the Senate's "advice and consent" was required for removal of officers of the United States, as well as the proposition that the President could only remove officers for cause.

7.16.   In *Humphrey's Executor v. United States,* 295 U.S. 602 (1935), the Court held that: Federal Trade Commission (FTC) members (a/k/a "commissioners") are not deemed to be "officers" of the United States; Congress can limit the President's power to remove a commissioner to instances involving "inefficiency, neglect of duty or malfeasance in office"; an FTC commissioner is different than an "officer" of the United States because, in addition to exercising executive functions, he also exercises legislative and judicial functions; and Congress can limit the President's power to remove FTC commissioners in an effort to limit the coercive influence that might threaten their independence.

7.17. In *Morrison v. Olson*, 487 U.S. 654 (1988), the Court held that an independent counsel is an "inferior officer" of the United States. As a result, Congress could prohibit removal of the counsel except for cause.

7.18. In *Buckley v. Valeo*, 424 U.S. 1 (1976), the Court held that Congress, in an effort to ensure that the Commission functioned in a fair and impartial manner, could reserve to itself the right to appoint some members of the Federal Election Commission (FEC). The holding in *Humphrey's Executor v. United States*, 295 U.S. 602 (1935), which treated FTC commissioners as different than "officers" of the United States provided the basis for allowing the Congress to exercise control over the appointment of some FEC members.

8.1. **Answer (D) is the best answer.**

Answers (A), (B), and (C) are all correct. Agencies conduct inspections, requiring the filing of reports, etc., for a variety of reasons including the following: to gain information that they need to set policy through the promulgation of rules and regulations; to keep Congress advised regarding various matters; to gain information needed to enforce regulatory requirements; and to gain information needed to prosecute companies for civil and criminal violations. *See* W. FUNK, S. SHAPIRO & R. WEAVER, ADMINISTRATIVE PRACTICE AND PROCEDURE: PROBLEMS AND CASES 568 (West, 2d ed. 1997). However, because Answer (D) incorporates each of the prior answers, it is the most correct.

8.2. **Answer (D) is the best answer.** Agencies perform inspections for a variety of reasons including the ones suggested in Answers (A), (B), and (C). *See* W. FUNK, S. SHAPIRO & R. WEAVER, ADMINISTRATIVE PRACTICE AND PROCEDURE: PROBLEMS AND CASES 506-67 (West, 2d ed. 1997).

Answers (A), (B), and (C) are all correct. However, because Answer (D) incorporates each of these answers, it is the most correct.

8.3. **Answer (C) is correct.** In *Camara v. Municipal Court*, 387 U.S. 523 (1967), the Court held that even though administrative inspections are conducted for health and safety reasons, the Fourth Amendment prohibition against "unreasonable searches and seizures" is fully applicable.

Answer (A) is incorrect because the Fourth Amendment prohibition against unreasonable searches and seizures does apply to administrative inspections. *Id.*

Answer (B) is incorrect because *Camara* did not hold that a warrant was not required. *Id.*

Answer (D) is incorrect. Because Answer (C) is correct, Answer (D), which states that "none of the above" is correct, is necessarily incorrect.

8.4. **Answer (D) is the best answer.** In *Camara*, the Court articulated each of the propositions stated in Answers (A), (B), and (C). *See Camara v. Municipal Court*, 387 U.S. 523 (1967).

Answers (A), (B), and (C) are all correct. As a result, Answer (D), which states that "all of the above" answers are correct, is the best answer.

8.5. **Answer (C) is correct.** Answer (C) is the most correct because in *Camara*, the Court held that, because administrative searches and inspections do not involve searches for evidence of criminal activity, the probable cause requirement can be modified to require only a reasonable inspection plan and proof that it is time to inspect under that plan (as opposed to the ordinary requirement of proof that the fruits, instrumentalities of evidence of crime, exist and can be found at the place to be searched). *See Camara v. Municipal Court*, 387 U.S. 523 (1967).

Answer (A) is incorrect because the Court did not hold that administrative inspections should be treated like any other search and that the warrant requirement should be strictly applied. *Id.*

Answer (B) is incorrect because the Court did compromise the warrant requirement by modifying the probable cause requirement. *Id.*

Answer (D) is incorrect. Because Answer (C) is correct, Answer (D), which states that "none of the above" is correct, is necessarily incorrect.

8.6.   **Answer (C) is correct** because, although the Fourth Amendment requires a warrant and probable cause in order to conduct an administrative inspection, few inspections are actually based on a warrant because the individual or business being inspected usually gives consent to the search. Indeed, many trade and industry groups advise their members to consent to searches absent unusual circumstances which might justify refusal. *See* W. FUNK, S. SHAPIRO & R. WEAVER, ADMINISTRATIVE PRACTICE AND PROCEDURE: PROBLEMS AND CASES 573 (West, 2d ed. 1997).

Answer (A) is incorrect because most administrative inspections are not conducted pursuant to a warrant. *Id.*

Answer (B) is incorrect because the Court did not regard the requirement of probable cause, in its strict sense, as essential. *Id.*

Answer (D) is incorrect. Because Answer (C) is correct, Answer (D), which states that "none of the above" is correct, is necessarily incorrect.

8.7.   **Answer (D) is the best answer.** In various decisions, the Court has upheld that all of these businesses (referred to in Answers (A), (B), and (C)) qualify as "closely regulated" businesses. Because Answer (D) incorporates all three of these answers, it is the best answer.

8.8.   In *Janis*, the Court held that, as a general rule, the exclusionary evidence rule does not apply in administrative proceedings because the costs of exclusion outweigh the bene fits. *United States v. Janis*, 428 U.S. 433 (1976). As a result, the general rule suggests that the exclusionary rule does not apply in the administrative context.

8.9.   In *United States v. Janis*, 428 U.S. 433 (1976), the United States Supreme Court held that, as a general rule, the exclusionary evidence rule does not apply in administrative proceedings because the costs of exclusion outweigh the benefits. In *Janis*, the evidence was seized by the police for use in criminal proceedings, but used by the IRS in civil proceedings, and the Court concluded that the police incentive to seize related to the criminal proceeding (and that little additional incentive existed to seize the evidence merely for use a civil enforcement proceeding). In this intra-agency context, the Court found that the benefits of exclusion (deterrence of police misconduct) were outweighed by the costs of exclusion (the loss of valuable evidence in the proceeding). As a result, the Court is most likely to apply the exclusionary rule in administrative proceedings when the benefits outweigh the costs (e.g., to an intra-agency violation). *See* W. Funk, S. Shapiro & R. Weaver, Administrative Practice and Procedure: Problems and Cases 585 (West, 2d ed. 1997).

8.10.   **Answer (C) is correct.** In *Janis*, the evidence was seized by the police for use in criminal proceedings, but used by the IRS in civil proceedings, and the Court concluded that the police incentive to seize related to the criminal proceeding (and that little additional incentive existed to seize the evidence merely for use a civil enforcement proceeding). In this intra-agency context, the Court found that the benefits of exclusion (deterrence of police misconduct) were outweighed by the costs of exclusion (the loss of valuable evidence in the proceeding). *United States v. Janis*, 428 U.S. 433 (1976). As a result, Answer (C) is correct.

Answer (A) is incorrect because the Court did not hold that there was very little benefit to be gained from applying the exclusionary rule in administrative proceedings. *Id.*

Answer (B) is incorrect because the Court did not hold that civil proceedings are less important than criminal proceedings. *Id.*

Answer (D) is incorrect. Because Answer (C) is correct, Answer (D), which states that "none of the above" is correct, is necessarily incorrect.

8.11.   **Answer (D) is the best answer.** In *Lopez-Mendoza*, the Court articulated all of the propositions set forth in Answers (A), (B), and (C). Because Answer (D) incorporates all of these propositions, it is the best answer. *INS v. Lopez-Mendoza*, 468 U.S 1032 (1984).

8.12.   **Answer (C) is correct** because, while statutory authorization is required, the authoriza tion can be explicit or implicit. *See* W. Funk, S. Shapiro & R. Weaver, Administrative Practice and Procedure: Problems and Cases 586 (West, 2d ed. 1997).

Answer (A) is incorrect because agencies do not have inherent authority to impose recordkeeping or reporting requirements. *Id.*

Answer (B) is incorrect because agencies do not have to hold explicit authorization to impose recordkeeping or reporting requirements. *Id.*

Answer (D) is incorrect. Because Answer (C) is correct, Answer (D), which states that "none of the above" is correct, is necessarily incorrect.

8.13.   **Answer (D) is the best answer.**

Answers (A), (B), and (C) are all correct because the Paperwork Reduction Act requires all of these things. 44 U.S.C. §§ 3501, *et seq.* Because Answer (D) incorporates all three of the prior answers, it is the best answer.

8.14.   **Answer (B) is correct** because, as a general rule, courts require nothing more than the requirement of reasonableness. *See* W. Funk, S. Shapiro & R. Weaver, Administrative Practice and Procedure: Problems and Cases 586–88 (West, 2d ed. 1997).

   Answer (A) is incorrect because probable cause is not required for a subpoena. *Id.*

   Answer (C) is incorrect because a subpoena can be issued even though it arguably involves a so-called "fishing expedition." *Id.*

   Answer (D) is incorrect. Because Answer (B) is correct, Answer (D), which states that "none of the above" is correct, is necessarily incorrect.

8.15.   In *Whalen v. Roe*, 429 U.S. 589 (1977), although the Court refused to quash the production of information on privacy grounds, the Court concluded that privacy rights might limit the government's ability to acquire information.

8.16.   In general, the Fifth Amendment privilege against self-incrimination does not apply to corporations. *See Wilson v. United States*, 221 U.S. 361 (1911); *Hale v. Henkel*, 201 U.S. 43 (1906). In addition, it does not provide broad protection against subpoenas. *See United States v. Doe*, 465 U.S. 605 (1984); *Shapiro v. United States*, 335 U.S. 1 (1948). There are only limited situations when the privilege provides protection to individuals. *See Marchetti v. United States*, 390 U.S. 39 (1968).

8.17.   **Answer (A) is correct.** The Privilege can be used to resist the production of documents when the mere act of production, as opposed to the contents of the documents, would incriminate the person producing the documents.

   Answer (B) is incorrect. Under *Securities and Exchange Commission v. Dresser Industries, Inc.*, 628 F.2d 1368 (D.C. Cir.1980), the Privilege does not provide regulated entities with the basis for objecting to being required to simultaneously defend both civil and criminal proceedings.

   Answer (C) is incorrect. The privilege applies in administrative proceedings just as it applies in administrative proceedings.

   Answer (D) is incorrect. Because Answers (B) and (C) are incorrect, Answer (D), which states that "all of the above" answers are correct, is necessarily incorrect.

9.1.   **Answer (B) is correct** because agencies, upon any request for records which reasonably describes such records and is made in accordance with published rules stating the time, place, fees (if any), and procedures to be followed, shall make the records promptly available to any person." *See* W. Funk, S. Shapiro & R. Weaver, Administrative Practice and Procedure: Problems and Cases 625–27 (West, 2d ed., 1997).

Answer (A) is incorrect in that agencies can impose reasonable charges for searching and copying documents. *Id.*

Answer (C) is incorrect because it states that "both of the above" answers are correct.

Answer (D) is incorrect because it states that "neither of the above" answers is correct.

9.2.   **Answer (D) is the best answer.**

Answers (A), (B), and (C) are all correct. *See* W. Funk, S. Shapiro & R. Weaver, Administrative Practice and Procedure: Problems and Cases 625–27 (West, 2d ed. 1997). However, Answer (D), which incorporates each of these answers, is the best answer.

9.3.   **Answer (D) is the best answer.**

Answers (A), (B), and (C) are all correct. *See* W. Funk, S. Shapiro & R. Weaver, Administrative Practice and Procedure: Problems and Cases 641–55 (West, 2d ed., 1997). However, Answer (D), which incorporates each of these answers, is the best answer because all of these exceptions apply under the FOIA.

9.4.   **Answer (B) is correct** because agencies can charges fees designed to allow them to recover the direct cost of searching, duplicating, and reviewing commercial requests. *See* W. Funk, S. Shapiro & R. Weaver, Administrative Practice and Procedure: Problems and Cases 627–28 (West, 2d ed., 1997).

Answer (A) is incorrect because, under the original FOIA, agencies could impose fair and equitable charges for the cost of searching for and producing documents. *Id.*

Answer (C) is incorrect because an agency is not required under FOIA to resolve unanswered questions and produce documents that do not exist. *Id.*

Answer (D) is incorrect. Because Answer (B) is correct, Answer (D), which states that "none of the above" is correct, is necessarily incorrect.

9.5.   **Answer (B) is correct** because there is an automatic right to seek judicial review. *See* W. FUNK, S. SHAPIRO & R. WEAVER, ADMINISTRATIVE PRACTICE AND PROCEDURE: PROBLEMS AND CASES 628–29 (West, 2d ed. 1997).

Answer (A) is incorrect. The statement that judicial review is precluded is simply wrong. *Id.*

Answer (C) is incorrect. The statement that an individual must ask the agency to reconsider before seeking judicial review is simply inaccurate. *Id.*

Answer (D) is incorrect. Because Answer (B) is correct, Answer (D), which states that "none of the above" is correct, is necessarily incorrect.

9.6.   **Answer (D) is the best answer.**

Answers (A), (B), and (C) are all correct. *See* W . FUNK, S. SHAPIRO & R. WEAVER, ADMINISTRATIVE PRACTICE AND PROCEDURE: PROBLEMS AND CASES 628–29 (West, 2d ed. 1997). However, Answer (D), which incorporates each of these answers, is the best answer.

9.7.   **Answer (D) is the best answer.**

Answers (A), (B), and (C) are all correct. *See* W. FUNK, S. SHAPIRO & R. WEAVER, ADMINISTRATIVE PRACTICE AND PROCEDURE: PROBLEMS AND CASES 623–31 (West, 2d ed. 1997). However, Answer (D), which incorporates each of these answers, is the best answer. All of these groups are entitled to use the FOIA.

9.8.   **Answer (C) is correct** because no showing of need is required. *See* W. FUNK, S. SHAPIRO & R. WEAVER, ADMINISTRATIVE PRACTICE AND PROCEDURE: PROBLEMS AND CASES 623–31 (West, 2d ed. 1997).

Answers (A) and (B) are incorrect because they suggest that a showing of need is necessary. *Id.*

Answer (D) is incorrect. Because Answer (C) is correct, Answer (D), which states that "none of the above" is correct, is necessarily incorrect.

9.9.   **Answer (B) is correct** because a reasonable description is all that is required. *See* W. FUNK, S. SHAPIRO & R. WEAVER, ADMINISTRATIVE PRACTICE AND PROCEDURE: PROBLEMS AND CASES 623–26 (West, 2d ed., 1997).

Answer (A) is incorrect because something more than a general description is required.

Answer (C) is incorrect because it states that both Answer (A) and Answer (B) are correct.

Answer (D) is incorrect. Because Answer (B) is correct, Answer (D), which states that "none of the above" is correct, is necessarily incorrect.

10.1. **Answer (A) is a true statement.** Courts in the United States have traditionally followed the "American rule" regarding attorney's fees, meaning that each party generally must bear its own legal expenses. However, numerous statutes exist which provide a means for recovery of some or all of the costs, fees and other expenses, including attorney's fees.

Answer (B) is not true. Contingency fee arrangements are permitted; and often used in cases where the claimant is bringing a suit against a federal agency to recover a monetary benefit.

Answer (C) is not true. Fee shifting provisions are often enacted by Congress to encourage certain types of litigation. One means for encouraging the enforcement of federal regulatory schemes is to allow private citizens to bring lawsuits against the federal agency and to include therein specific authorization to award costs and attorney fees, when appropriate, to a prevailing or substantially prevailing party.

Answer (D) is not true for the reasons noted above.

10.2. **Answer (D) is the least accurate statement.** The Act authorizes awards in "adversary adjudications." *See* § 504(a)(1). Further, the Act defines an "adversary adjudication" as including only adjudications "in which the position of the United States is represented by counsel or otherwise. . . ." *See* § 504(b)(1)(C). However, the Act also defines "adversary adjudication" as meaning only "formal" adjudication (i.e., adjudications under § 554 of the APA.) *See* § 504(a)(1)(C). The Supreme Court has construed this language narrowly and as not rendering the Act applicable in informal adjudications that use procedures mirroring APA's formal procedures. *See Ardestani v. INS*, 502 U.S. 129 (1991).

Answer (A) is not the least accurate statement. 28 U.S.C. § 2412(d) specifically authorizes the award that may be made in an action for judicial review of agency action and an adversary adjudication. *See* § 2412(d)(1) & (d)(3). Subsection (d) not only waives the sovereign immunity of the United States, but it also creates a new basis for an award of attorney's fees beyond the common law and specific statutory exception to the American rule.

Answer (B) is not the least accurate statement. The Act authorizes an award of attorney's fees in "any civil action brought by or against the United States or any agency or any official of the United States acting in his or her official capacity. . . ." *See* 28 U.S.C. § 2412(b)(1). Subsection (b) provides a general waiver of sovereign immunity, and makes the federal agencies liable for fees under common-law and statutory fee-shifting rule to the same extent as any other party.

Answer (C) is not the least accurate statement. The Act authorizes awards in certain agency adjudications, but § 504(b)(1)(C) expressly excludes an adjudication for the purpose of granting or renewing a license.

10.3. **Answer (A) is an accurate statement.** Section 2412(d)(1)(A) provides that a court "shall award to a prevailing party" fees and costs incurred by that party in the civil action, including proceedings for judicial review "unless the court finds that the position of the United States was substantially justified or that special circumstances make an award unjust." Section 2412(d)(1)(B) requires a proper and timely application for the award. Here, because the district court reversed the agency's denial of benefits, the claimant is a prevailing party.

Answer (B) is not an accurate statement. Section 2412(b) provides that a court "may award reasonable fees and expenses of attorneys, in addition to costs," to a prevailing party. However, this subsection of § 2412 does not include the proviso regarding a substantially justified position by the agency. Further, subsection (b) does not create a new basis for the award of attorney's fees. So, even if the position of the agency is sufficiently justified, a court "may" award attorney's fees to a prevailing party — if a common law rule or a distinct statutory provision provides an exception to the American rule.

Answer (C) is not an accurate statement. Section 2412(a)(1) provides that a "judgment for costs . . . not including the fees and expenses of attorneys may be awarded to the prevailing party in any civil action brought by or against the United States or any agency. . . ." However, this subsection of § 2412 does not include the proviso regarding a substantially justified position by the agency. So, even if the position of the agency is sufficiently justified, a court "may" award costs to a prevailing party — if it is appropriate.

Answer (D) is not an accurate statement. In certain cases, such as an award by a federal court in an action for judicial review, the court may include in that award fees and other expenses incurred in the proceeding before the agency. However, § 2412(d)(3) limits such an award to cases in which the review is of an "adversary adjudication" as defined by § 504(c)(1)(C) — i.e., an adjudication in which formal APA procedures were required. *But see Sullivan v. Hudson*, 490 U.S. 877 (1989) (holding that a fee claimant may recover attorneys fees through subsection (d) for even non-adversarial administrative proceedings — if such proceedings are "intimately connected" to an ongoing judicial proceeding (e.g., those proceeding following a remand to the agency if the court retains jurisdiction and contemplates the entry of a judgment upon completion of the administrative proceedings)).

10.4. **Answer (C) is an accurate statement** for the reasons noted above. The Court in *Pierce* adopted the view that the phrase "substantially justified" should be construed to mean "justified to a degree that could satisfy a reasonable person." *Pierce v. Underwood*, 487 U.S. 552 (1988).

Answer (A) is not an accurate statement. In *Pierce v. Underwood*, 487 U.S. 552 (1988), the Supreme Court considered the standard set out in 28 U.S.C. § 2412(d)(1)(A), and adopted a standard that requires greater justification than this formulation of the standard would require. However, the Court also explained that the accepted understanding of the "substantial evidence" standard of review suggested that the phrase "substantially justified" should not be construed as requiring "a large or considerable amount of evidence;" but, rather, should be construed similarly to the standard of requiring "such relevant evidence as a reasonable mind might accept as adequate to support a conclusion."

Answer (B) is not an accurate statement for the reasons noted above.

Answer (D) is incorrect because Answer (C) is an accurate statement.

10.5. **Answer (C) is an accurate statement.** Section 504(a)(2) provides that, when the agency "appeals the underlying merits of the adversary proceeding, no decision on an application for fees and other expenses . . . shall be made . . . until a final and unreviewable decision is rendered by the court on appeal[;] or until the underlying merits of the case have been finally determined pursuant to the appeal [e.g., determined upon remand to the agency for decision in light of the appeal]."

Answer (A) is not an accurate statement. Section 504(a)(1) does provide that the agency "that conducts an adversary adjudication shall award, to a prevailing party other than the United States, fees and other expenses incurred by that party in connection with that proceeding. . . ." However, § 504(a)(1)'s mandate is qualified; the award must be provided "unless the adjudicative officer of the agency finds that the position of the agency was substantially justified or that special circumstances make an award unjust."

Answer (B) is not an accurate statement. Section 504(a)(2) requires a party to submit to the agency "an application" for the award; § 504(a)(1) requires the agency to make the award, unless the agency finds that the agency position was substantially justified; and § 504(a)(3) authorizes the adjudicative officer of the agency to reduce the award or to deny the award. However, the application must be proper and the agency can defer if the agency appeals the merits of the decision. First, the application must satisfy certain statutory requirements. Section 504(a)(2) requires a party seeking an award to submit to the agency "an application which shows that the party is a prevailing party and is eligible to receive an award, and the amount sought. . . ." Further, § 504(a)(2) also requires an allegation that the position of the agency was not substantially justified. Second, as explained below, an appeal requires deferment of the award determination.

Answer (D) is incorrect because neither Answer (A) nor Answer (B) is an accurate statement.

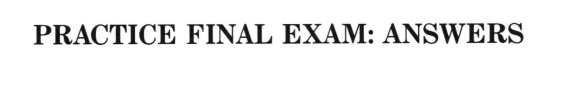

PRACTICE FINAL EXAM: ANSWERS

1.1.   **Answer (D) is the best answer.** In *Morisson v. Olson*, 487 U.S. 654 (1988), the Court articulated all three of the propositions contained in Answers (A), (B), and (C). However, since Answer (D) incorporates all three of these propositions, it is the most accurate answer.

1.2.   **Answer (A) is an accurate statement.** Section 2(b) provides that coordinated review of agency rulemaking is necessary to ensure that regulations are consistent with applicable law, the President's priorities, and principles set forth in the Executive Order. OMB is given authority to carry out that review; and ORIA is an office within OMB with expertise concerning regulatory issues.

Answer (B) is an accurate statement. Section 1(a) provides that agencies should assess all costs and benefits of available regulatory alternatives and should select regulatory approaches that maximize net benefits. Further, § 6(a)(3)(B) directs each agency to provide to OIRA, for a significant regulatory action, an assessment of the potential costs and benefits of the action.

Answer (C) is not an accurate statement. Section 1(a) provides that agencies should assess all costs and benefits of available regulatory alternatives and should select regulatory approaches that maximize net benefits. Further, § 6(a)(3)(B) directs each agency to provide to OIRA, for a significant regulatory action, an assessment of the potential costs and benefits of the action. Section 6(b)(3) requires the Administrator of OIRA, upon returning a proposed regulatory action to the agency for "further reconsideration," to provide a written explanation for the return. But, that section also authorizes the agency head who disagrees with the basis for the return to inform the Administrator in writing. Section 7 clarifies that, if OIRA and the agency cannot resolve a disagreement, the President, in consultation with the Chief of Staff and other regulatory policy advisors, may resolve the conflict.

Answer (D) is an accurate statement. Section 5(a) directs agencies to submit to OIRA a program under which the agency will periodically review its existing, significant regulations to determine whether any such regulations should be modified or eliminated so as to make the regulatory program more effective, less burdensome, or more in-line with presidential priorities.

1.3.   **Answer (A) is correct.** The APA requires formal trial-like procedures only when the statute authorizing the rulemaking requires the determination to be made "on the record" after an opportunity for a hearing; and Congress has rarely used the language necessary to trigger formal APA procedures for the promulgation of rules. *See Allegheny-Ludlum Steel Corp. v. United States*, 406 U.S. 742 (1972);

Florida East Coast Railroad Co. v. United States, 410 U.S. 224 (1973).

Answer (B) is not correct. The APA requires formal trial-like procedures only when the statute authorizing the adjudication requires the determination to be made "on the record" after an opportunity for a hearing. *See, e.g., Chemical Waste Management, Inc. v. EPA*, 873 F.2d 1477 (D.C. Cir. 1989) (using the *Chevron* analysis to determine whether Congress intended to require formal APA procedures through use of the term "hearing").

Answer (C) is not correct because, even if formal APA protections are not required, the agency action must comport with due process. *See, e.g., Goldberg v. Kelly*, 397 U.S. 254 (1970).

Answer (D) is not correct. Congress may require the agency to follow procedures following somewhere between the APA's formal trial-like procedures and the APA's informal notice and comment procedures. That is, the agency may be required to follow what is sometimes referred to as "hybrid" procedures.

1.4.   The primary safeguard, arguably, is the requirement of public disclosure of all documents exchanged between OIRA and the agency during the review by ORIA. Section 6(b)(4) provides that, after a regulatory action has been issued to the public (or after the agency has announced a decision not to issue a regulatory action), OIRA must make available to the public all documents exchanged between OIRA and the agency during the review by OIRA. This would require disclosure of any written explanations for a decision by OIRA to return a regulatory action to an agency for reconsideration; as well as written responses from the agency head if the agency disagrees with the reasons cited by OIRA. Accordingly, the public will be able to ascertain the substantive changes between the rule as it was submitted to OIRA and the final rule, and which changes were due to OIRA recommendations.

A secondary safeguard, arguably, is the requirement in section 4(d) that the Administrator of OIRA convene a regulatory "working group." The working group serves as a forum to assist agencies in analyzing regulatory issues. Section 4(d) provides that the working group shall consist of representatives of the heads of each agency that the Administrator determines to have significant domestic regulatory responsibilities. Because the group is comprised of agency heads, it may help temper the power of the Director of OMB or the Administrator of OIRA. An additional safeguard, perhaps, is the vesting of final authority for resolving conflicts between the agency and OIRA with the President, as opposed to the Director of OMB or the Administrator of OIRA. *See* Section 7. This provision technically enhances the power of the President. However, the President may need to show restraint in exercising that power given that a decision regarding a significant regulatory action can be linked directly to the President, as opposed to the administrative state generally.

1.5.   **Answer (C) is an accurate statement.** Section 2412(a)(1) provides that a "judgment for costs . . . not including the fees and expenses of attorneys may be awarded to the prevailing party in any civil action brought by or against the United

States or any agency. . . ." Further, this subsection does not exclude the United States from such an award; and does not include the proviso regarding a substantially justified position by non-prevailing party. So, the court may award costs to the agency.

Answer (A) is not an accurate statement. Section 2412(d)(1)(A) provides that a court shall award to a prevailing party "other than the United States" fees and costs incurred by that party in the civil action, including proceedings for judicial review; "unless the court finds that the position of the United States was substantially justified or that special circumstances make an award unjust." Further, § 2412(d)(2)(C) defines the "United States" as including "any agency and any official of the United States acting in his or her official capacity." Thus, a court may not award under subsection (d) fees and other expenses to the agency.

Answer (B) is not an accurate statement. Section 2412(b) provides that a court "may award reasonable fees and expenses of attorneys, in addition to costs," to a prevailing party. Further, this subsection does not exclude the United States from such an award. However, this subsection of § 2412 is not viewed as having created any substantive rights. Subsection (b) provides only a waiver of sovereign immunity of the United States. Thus, whether a court "may" award attorneys fees to the agency as a prevailing party depends on whether such an award is authorized by some other statute or rule.

Answer (D) is incorrect because Answer (C) is an accurate statement.

1.6.   **Answer (C) is an accurate statement.** Courts will review a denial, but the review is very deferential and courts will hesitate to second-guess an agency's decision, especially if the decision hinges on priority setting among important agency concerns. *See Northern Spotted Owl v. Hodel,* 716 F. Supp. 479 (W.D. Wash. 1988).

Answer (A) is not an accurate statement. Section 553(e) provides that an agency must give prompt notice of a denial. Further, § 706 allows a reviewing court to compel agency action unlawfully withheld or unreasonably delayed, and § 551(13) defines "agency action" as including failure to act.

Answer (B) is not an accurate statement. As noted, § 706 allows a reviewing court to compel agency action unlawfully withheld or unreasonably delayed, and § 551(13) defines "agency action" as including failure to act. A failure to act on a petition for rulemaking may become unreasonable after several years. *See Telecommunications Research & Action Center v. FCC,* 750 F.2d 70 (D.C. Cir. 1984).

Answer (D) is not an accurate statement because § 553 provides that, along with a denial of a written petition, the agency must provide a brief statement of the grounds for the denial.

1.7.   **Answer (B) is an accurate statement.** Section 553(d) specifies that the required publication of a substantive rule "shall be made not less than 30 days before its effective date" — unless the substantive rule falls within the exception in § 553(d)(1). Section 553(d)(1) exempts from the 30 day requirement substantive rules which grant or recognize an exemption or relieve a restriction. The new rule is a prohibition on certain conduct and does not fall within the § 553(d)(1) exception. Thus, given the February 3 publication date, the new ban on snowmobiles could not have an effective date of March 1 or before.

Answer (A) is not an accurate statement. As discussed below, publication in the *FederalRegister* is not the only requirement relating to the effectiveness of an agency rule.

Answer (C) is not an accurate statement. Section 552(a) creates an exception for persons who have actual and timely notice of the terms of rules; and allows an agency to enforce or apply a rule against persons with such notice. However, the exception in § 552(a) allows an agency to use or apply a rule that was required to be published in the Federal Register but which was not so published. Section 552(a) does not specify that it allows an agency to circumvent the 30 day notice period required by § 553(d).

Answer (D) is incorrect since Answer (B) is an accurate statement.

1.8.   The term "executive agencies" is often used to refer to "departments" and agencies within "departments." Departments and agencies within departments are generally headed by persons who are appointed by the President, with the advice and consent of the Senate, and who serve at the pleasure of the President. This means that these agency heads can be terminated by the President. Accordingly, the President can exert greater influence over "executive agencies." Independent agencies are not part of a department. Further, they are not headed by a single person, but, rather, are headed by a multi-member group such as a commission, board, or council. Members of the commission, board, or council have greater insulation from presidential influence because they generally can be removed only "for cause;" and political disagreement generally is insufficient cause for removal. Additionally, although the President may have authority to appoint members of the group heading independent agencies, these members generally serve for a term of years; and the terms are staggered so that a President generally is unable to replace all members.

1.9.   **Answer (C) is the correct answer.** A decision to tax and the amount of a tax is more akin to rulemaking — even if the tax affects only certain taxpayers. Section 551(4) specifies that a "rule" sometimes may constitute a statement of "particular" applicability.

Answer (A) is an agency adjudication. An agency is any authority of the government (§ 551(1)), and this action is an adjudication. Section 551(7) defines "adjudication" as an "agency process for the formulation of an order." Section 551(6) defines "order" as the "whole or part of a final disposition . . . of an agency in a matter other than rule mak ing but including licensing." Section 551(5) defines "rulemaking" as the "agency process for formulating, amending, or repealing a rule." A "rule" is defined by § 551(4) as "the whole or part of an agency statement of general . . . applicability and future affect. . . ." An "adjudication" then, is the agency process for formulating a decision of "particular" applicability and "present" effect. The police officer made a determination about a particular car and with a present (or more immediate) effect.

Answer (B) is an agency adjudication. It is a determination about a particular entity's authority to participate in a federal program and it has a present (or more immediate) effect.

Answer (D) is an agency adjudication. It is a determination about a particular individual's right to continue providing flight instruction.

1.10. In a long line of cases, the Court has upheld warrantless inspections of closely regulated businesses. *See, e.g., New York v. Burger*, 482 U.S. 691 (1987); *Donovan v. Dewey*, 452 U.S. 594 (1981); *United States v. Biswell*, 406 U.S. 311 (1972); *Colonnade Catering Corp. v. United States*, 397 U.S. 72 (1970). Warrantless searches can also be permitted with consent. *See Schneckloth v. Bustamonte*, 412 U.S. 218 (1973).

1.11. **Answer (C) is the best answer.** Although the standing doctrine is grounded in Article III's case and controversy requirement, it is also grounded in prudential considerations. Even if Article III is satisfied, the Court can still decline to hear the case. *See Sierra Club v. Morton*, 405 U.S. 727 (1972).

Answers (A) and (B) are correct, but neither is as complete or as accurate an answer as Answer (C).

Answer (D) is incorrect. Because Answer (C) is correct, Answer (D), which states "none of the above" is correct, is necessarily incorrect.

1.12. **Answer (B) is correct** because the due process clause is often applied to retroactive laws and judicial decisions, as well as to administrative rules, decisions and policies.

Answer (A) is incorrect because retroactive criminal laws are primarily prohibited by the Ex Post Facto Clause of the United States Constitution, and the concept of retroactivity extends well beyond retroactive criminal laws. *See* Russell L. Weaver, *Retroactive Regulatory Interpretations: An Analysis of Judicial Responses*, 61 Notre Dame L. Rev. 167 (1986). Moreover, while retroactive criminal laws might also be prohibited by the due process clause, the primary resort is to the Ex Post Facto Clause. *Id.*

Answer (C) is incorrect because legislation is rarely applied retroactively.

Answer (D) is obviously incorrect.

1.13. **Answer (C) is correct.** Answer (C) correctly states the current state of the law: "In determining what Congress may do in seeking assistance from another branch, the extent and character of that assistance must be fixed according to common sense and the inherent necessities of government coordination." *See Mistretta v. United States*, 488 U.S. 361 (1989).

Answer (A) is incorrect because it is not accurate to state that the "integrity and maintenance of the system of government ordained by the Constitution precludes

Congress from delegating legislative power to another branch of government." *See* W. FUNK, S. SHAPIRO & R. WEAVER, ADMINISTRATIVE PRACTICE AND PROCEDURE: PROBLEMS AND CASES 506-67 (West, 2d ed. 1997).

Answer (B) is incorrect because separation of powers principles, and check and balances principles, do not prohibit Congress from delegating power to other branches of government. *Id.*

Answer (D) is incorrect. Because Answer (C) is correct, Answer (D), which states that "none of the above" is correct, is necessarily incorrect.

1.14. **Answer (A) is correct.** Although the Private Express Statute might have been designed to prohibit what the USPS did, the Court held that postal employees did not have standing to raise the issue. *Air Courier Conference of America v. American Postal Workers Union*, AFL-CIO, 498 U.S. 517 (1991). The statute was not designed to protect them, and therefore they were not within the statute's "zone of interest." *Id.*

Answer (B) is incorrect. Because Answer (B) directly contradicts Answer (A), and states a proposition directly contradictory to the holding in *Air Courier*, it is necessarily incorrect. *Id.*

Answer (C) is incorrect because the Court did not go so far as to suggest that employees would never have standing.

Answer (D) is incorrect. Because Answer (B) is correct, Answer (D), which says that "none of the above" is correct, is necessarily incorrect since one of the answers is correct.

1.15. **Answer (C) is correct.** Delegations are permissible, but they must be accompanied by an intelligible principle to which the person or body authorized to [exercise the authority] is directed to conform. *See Mistretta v. United States*, 488 U.S. 361 (1989).

Answer (A) is incorrect. It is not necessary to have the assent of all three branches of government in order to make a delegation of power.

Answer (B) is incorrect. Under *Panama Refining* and *Schechter*, the Court seemed to require Congress to provide specific guidance so that the coordinate branch of government is called upon to do no more than implement, rather than formulate, policy.

Answer (D) is incorrect. Because Answer (C) is correct, Answer (D), which states that "none of the above" is correct, is necessarily incorrect.

1.16. The case is ripe for review. *See National Automatic Laundry and Dry Cleaning Council v. Shultz*, 443 F.2d 689 (D.C. Cir. 1971). The letter places the association's members on the horns of a dilemma; either they comply with the letter or they face sanctions.

1.17. **Answer (C) is correct** because Congress cannot reserve to itself the power to remove officers of the United States. *See Bowsher v. Synar*, 478 U.S. 714 (1986).

Answer (A) is incorrect because the Court did not hold that "Congress may supervise officers of the United States in their execution of the laws of the United States." *Id.*

Answer (B) is incorrect because the Court did not hold that "Congress may reserve to itself the power to remove officers of the United States." *Id.*

Answer (D) is incorrect. Because Answer (C) is correct, Answer (D), which states that "none of the above" is correct, is necessarily incorrect.

1.18. The Freedom of Information Act is primarily a disclosure statute and cannot be used to prevent the disclosure of information. *See Chrysler Corp. v. Brown*, 441 U.S. 281 (1979). As a result, the objection is invalid.

1.19. **Answer (C) is correct** because neither Congress nor the courts usually require that agencies use either legislative or adjudicative requirements. As a result, agencies impose such requirements in a variety of ways. *See* W. Funk, S. Shapiro & R. Weaver, Administrative Practice and Procedure: Problems and Cases 586–88 (West, 2d ed. 1997).

Answer (A) is incorrect because agencies are not required to create recordkeeping and reporting requirements legislatively using notice and comment procedures. *Id.*

Answer (B) is incorrect because agencies are not required to create recordkeeping and reporting requirements using adjudicative procedures. *Id.*

Answer (D) is incorrect. Because Answer (C) is correct, Answer (D), which states that "none of the above" is correct, is necessarily incorrect.

1.20. **Answer (B) is correct.** If the party in an agency proceeding is a business, § 504(b)(1)(B) and 28 U.S.C. 2412(d)(2)(B) limit the definition of party to a business with a net worth that did not exceed $7 million at the time the adversary adjudication was initiated and which had no more than 500 employees at the time the adversary adjudication was initiated. Therefore, assuming the business had 800 employees at the time the adversary adjudication was initiated, the business would be ineligible to recover the fees and other expenses allowed under the Equal Access to Justice Act.

Answer (A) is incorrect. Section 504(b)(1)(B) defines party as a person named or admitted as a party in an agency proceeding (*see* § 551(3)), and, if the party is an individual, one whose net worth did not exceed $2 million at the time the adversary adjudication was initiate. *See* § 504(b)(1)(B); 28 U.S.C. 2412(d)(2)(B).

Answer (C) is incorrect. Section 504(b)(1)(B) and 28 U.S.C. 2412(d)(2)(B) define party as a person named or admitted as a party in an agency proceeding (*see* § 551(3)), and, if the party is an IRS § 501(c)(3) tax-exempt organization, the organization may recover costs and attorneys fees regardless of its net worth.

Answer (D) is incorrect. If the party in an agency proceeding is a unit of local government, the limitations of § 504(b)(1)(B) and 28 U.S.C. 2412(d)(2)(B) apply. The unit of government must have a net worth that did not exceed $7 million at the time the adversary adjudication was initiated and it must not have had more than 500 employees at the time the adversary adjudication was initiated.

1.21.   **Answer (B) is the most sound judicial response.** The key inquiry in deciding whether a rule falls within the exception for rules of "agency organization, procedure or practice" is whether the rule is essentially a "housekeeping measure" or a rule that alters merely the manner in which parties present themselves to the agency; or whether the rule affects, in a more substantive way, the rights and interests of regulated parties. The rule at issue here affects the rights of the Hospital, but not in a sufficiently substantive way (for the reasons noted below). Moreover, the rule does not change Medicare's substantive reimbursement standards but, rather, governs merely the timing of submissions and thus the efficiency of the appeals process. *See Inova Alexandria Hosp.* v. *Shalala*, 244 F.3d 342 (4th Cir. 2001).

   Answer (A) is incorrect. Although an exception to notice and comment procedures exists for rules that merely prescribe the manner in which the parties present themselves to the agency, the exception does not hinge on the concept of impracticality. *See* APA § 553(b)(3)(A) & (B).

   Answer (C) is incorrect. The right to an appeal granted by the Medicare Act is a "substantive" right. Further, although Congress also granted authority to the Board to establish "procedures" to implement the provider right to appeals, procedural rules often have an impact on substantive rights. In cases such as this, the issue is whether the effect on the substantive right to a hearing is sufficiently grave so that notice and comment may be deemed necessary as a safeguard. Here, the interest impacted by the rule is a hospital's right to an unlimited time within which to submit its "position papers." Courts would not likely find that right to be so weighty that public notice and comment would be necessary. *See JEM Broadcasting Co.* v. *F.C.C.*, 22 F.3d 320 (D.C. Cir. 1994) (holding that a license applicant's right to notice and an opportunity to correct errors in the license application was not so significant as to have required the agency to use notice and comment procedures for a procedural rule eliminating that right).

   Answer (D) is incorrect. The Court of Appeals for the District of Columbia in an early case suggested that an agency's adoption of a comprehensive adjudication scheme required notice and comment procedures because the rule encoded a value judgment on the appropriate balance between a defendant's rights to adjudicatory procedures and the agency's interest in efficient prosecution. *See Air Transport Ass'n of America* v. *Department of Transportation*, 900 F.2d 369 (D.C. Cir. 1990). However in the *JEM Broadcasting* case, the court backed away from that narrow view of the exception for rules of "procedure," in favor of the reasoning discussed relating to Answer (C). *See JEM Broadcasting Co.* v. *F.C.C.*, 22 F.3d 320 (D.C. Cir. 1994).

1.22.   **Answer (C) is correct.** There are limited exceptions under the FOIA. Answer (C) states one of them. *See* W. FUNK, S. SHAPIRO & R. WEAVER, ADMINISTRATIVE PRACTICE AND PROCEDURE: PROBLEMS AND CASES 627–28 (West, 2d ed. 1997).

Answer (A) is incorrect because no distinction is made between citizens and noncitizens. *Id.*

Answer (B) is incorrect because there is no exemption for "commercial entities that show special need." *Id.*

Answer (D) is incorrect. Because Answer (C) is correct, Answer (D), which states that "none of the above" is correct, is necessarily incorrect.

1.23 **Answer (B) is an accurate statement.** The Court has clarified, in *Mead* and *Gonzales*, that *Chevron* deference "is warranted only 'when it appears that Congress delegated authority to the agency generally to make rules carrying the force of law, and that the agency interpretation claiming deference was promulgated in the exercise of that authority.'" *See Gonzales*, 546 U.S. 243 (2006); *Mead Corp.*, 533 U.S. 218 (2001). The facts of this question point to a delegation of authority to promulgate rules with the force of law, and support a finding that the regulation was promulgated in the exercise of that authority. The Court in *Mead* noted that *Chevron* deference has most often been applied to "the fruits of notice-and-comment rulemaking or formal adjudication." *See Estate of Gerson v. C.I.R.*, 507 F.3d 437 (6th Cir. 2007) (from which the facts of this questions were drawn).

Answer (A) is not an accurate statement. After *Mead* and *Gonzales*, the fact that a regulation constitutes an agency interpretation of the statute the agency is charged with implementing — even a regulation promulgated pursuant to notice and comment rulemaking — may not suffice for the application of *Chevron* deference.

Answer (C) is not an accurate statement. The Court, in *Chevron* and other cases, has emphasized that "step-one" of a case involving an agency's interpretation of a statute allows a court to apply traditional tools of statutory interpretation to decide whether Congress was silent or ambiguous as to the precise issue involved, or left a gap to be filled by the agency. Thus, if the plain language of the statute prohibits the agency's interpretation, no deference is due.

Answer (D) is not an accurate statement. In part, the statement is not accurate for the reason explained in relation to Answer (C); but it is also not accurate because, on the facts of this problem, the IRS has a strong argument that the regulation has the force of law.

1.24 This question raises the issue of whether the Johnsons' can assert a liberty interest that would trigger a right to procedural due process. On the facts of the question, the more precise issue is whether the Johnsons can satisfy the "stigma-plus" test recognized by the Supreme Court. A liberty interest may be implicated where a person's good name, reputation, honor, or integrity is at stake because of a state agency's actions, but only where a resulting stigma has foreclosed in some way a future pursuit qualifying for liberty interest protection and/or where the agency action has altered or extinguished a right or status previously recognized by state law. *See Paul v. Davis*, 424 U.S. 693 (1976); *Board of Regents v. Roth*, 408 U.S. 564 (1972); *Wisconsin v. Constantineau*, 400 U.S. 433 (1971). Cases satisfying the standard generally involve agency activity involving a finding of a disputed fact bearing on a person's honor or integrity, where that finding is made public pursuant to the regulatory scheme or will be accessible in such a way as to create a reasonable likelihood of an infringement on future rights.

Answer (C) is thus the accurate statement. *See Humphries v. County of Los Angeles*, 554 F.3d 1170, 1186–1192 (9th Cir. 2009) (concluding that the "plus-test" is satisfied if a regulatory scheme creates a stigma and a tangible burden on an individual's employment opportunities).

Answer (A) is not an accurate statement. Here, listing occurs if it is determined by an investigating agency that allegations of suspected child abuse or neglect is "not unfounded." Although the requisite finding is not that the person is guilty, it nonetheless is a finding that would call into question the person's good name, reputation, honor, or integrity.

Answer (B) is not an accurate statement. Although it is true that all future job opportunities may not be closed, many specific types of jobs will be foreclosed since the information is available for "pre-employment" background investigations (including specific opportunities that the Johnsons have stated that they want to pursue), and especially since many background checks are also required by state law.

Answer (D) is not an accurate statement. If the "plus-factors" are present, the availability of a defamation suit will not interfere with the finding of a liberty interest.

1.25   This question involves an assessment of an agency's procedures when a constitutionally protected liberty interest is at stake. When a liberty interest is at stake, an agency proceeding must provide sufficient procedural safeguards. In assessing the adequacy of procedural protections, courts weigh the factors set out in *Matthews v. Eldridge*, 424 U.S. 319 (1976), namely, the private interest affected; the risk of erroneous deprivation and value of additional safeguards; and the governmental interest, including fiscal and administrative burdens of additional procedures. The key procedures in the contested regulatory scheme are: the initial agency investigation and determination as to whether the allegations are "not unfounded"; the listing in the CACI by the DOJ; and the notification to the person about the listing. If allegations are subsequently found to be "unfounded," the DOJ has a duty to not retain a Child Abuse Report in the CACI. However, there is no mechanism built into the scheme whereby the agency or the DOJ would be compelled to reconsider a report, and no duty to remove persons from the CACI. Listed persons are limited to trying to spur the investigating agency to correct its reports, or relying on an inquiring agency to conduct an independent investigation.

Answer (D) is an appropriate judicial response. The response in (D) reflects the likelihood that the state could, without encountering undue costs, provide some additional procedures that would reduce the risk of error. Given the significant private interest and the high risk of error associated with the current procedure, a court should require more protections by the state. *See Humphries v. County of Los Angeles*, 554 F.3d 1170, 1193–1201 (9th Cir. 2009) (concluding that, although the state did not have to provide additional procedures prior to listing persons on the CACI, that state did need to provide "some kind of hearing" by which a listed person could challenge his inclusion).

Answers (A) and (B) do not reflect appropriate judicial responses. In this case, both the private interest and the state interest are strong, and thus the other factors become determinative.

Answer (C) also does not reflect an appropriate judicial response. The response described still fails to take into account the key factors of whether additional safeguards exist that would lessen the risk of error, and whether such additional procedures are feasible.

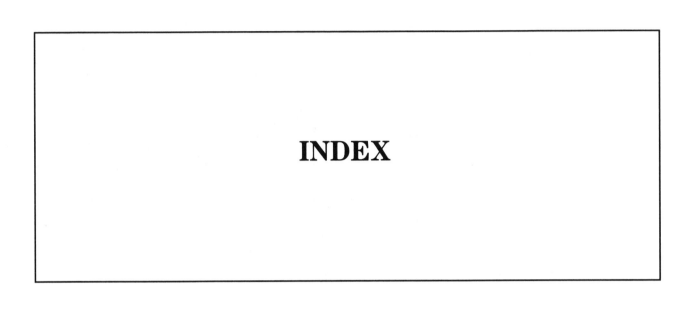

INDEX

INDEX

TOPIC	**QUESTION**